Without A Net

Preaching In The Paperless Pulpit

William H. Shepherd

CSS Publishing Company, Inc., Lima, Ohio

WITHOUT A NET

Library of Congress Cataloging-in-Publication Data

Shepherd, William H. (William Henry), 1957-
    Without a net : preaching in the paperless pulpit / William H. Shepherd.
      p. cm.
Includes bibliographical references.
    ISBN 0-7880-2307-1 (pbk. : alk. paper)
  1. Preaching. I. Title.
BV4211.3.S54 2004
251—dc22

                                                                    2003021047

For more information about CSS Publishing Company resources, visit our website at
www.csspub.com or e-mail us at custserv@csspub.com or call (800) 241-4056.

ISBN 0-7880-2307-1   PRINTED IN U.S.A.

To three preachers,
Mac Paterson, who inspired me,
Fred Craddock, who taught me,
and John Porter, who showed me the way.

Table Of Contents

Preface

For many preachers, the thought of speaking without a manuscript or notes makes them feel like a trapeze artist balancing on a high wire without a net. There you are, balancing delicately in the stratosphere, with nothing but you and your ballet shoes holding on for dear life. Why, oh why, did I not bring even a sliver of paper up here to catch me when I fall? The feeling is enhanced when one must climb stairs to reach a pulpit that does indeed look down on the congregation!

This book is written for preachers who need the control that writing a sermon manuscript provides, yet sense that simply reading the written words to the congregation will not do. We don't need surveys or scientific studies to tell us that modern people have a certain standard of eloquence, and reading a written speech doesn't cut it. The stretching, the yawns, the closed eyes, and afterwards, the polite "Nice sermon, Reverend," tell all. Our congregations watch television; they are used to listening to people who seem to speak naturally and conversationally without any prompts at all — yes, they may know all about the TelePrompTer, but the machine's genius is that it remains hidden, creating the illusion that the television star is speaking straight to them in their living room. While they may not say it, deep down inside they are dying to have someone in the pulpit address them in the same direct, conversational style.

The reasons for writing a sermon manuscript are obvious: we want to have precise control over what we are going to say. Yet in the pulpit, we want to be free to talk to the people, and not merely read something to them. We find ourselves in a bind, because while our written content may be thoughtful, the oral presentation makes it sound second-rate. Either we read our manuscripts, and put the room into a deep sleep, or we abandon our written prompts and find ourselves wandering off the subject or at a loss for words. We just aren't quick enough on our feet to preach extemporaneously.

This book will be most helpful to those preachers who need to prepare their sermons by writing a manuscript. It is *not* for those who are already quick on their feet, glib in a paperless pulpit. I've generally found that people who preach naturally without notes get much worse if they try to work with a manuscript. Nor is my method suitable for those who think that preaching without notes or manuscript will take less preparation time. Quite the opposite.

I am convinced that most of us who write out our sermons could do better if we would reconsider the sermon with the entire speaking process in view. We do not have to give up our manuscripts, but we will see them in a different light — as written helpers that take us a step closer to the sermon. The manuscripts are not the sermons themselves. The sermon is that which is said on Sunday from the pulpit; the words on the page merely help us get there.

If we begin with delivery in mind — and we picture ourselves preaching in a spontaneous style, without referring to notes or manuscript — we will go about the entire sermon preparation process, including both study and composition, in a completely different way. We must begin with the end in mind, which will change beginning, middle, and end.

Those who have been preaching for some time may wonder why this book takes them back to the basics for a review of the entire sermon-production process, as if they were mere beginners. The answer is not just that a little review is good for the soul. Rather, to preach in a new way involves thinking in a new way, from the beginning of the process. We cannot change the end result without changing our entire way of working. Thus, this book is a primer on the entire sermon process, suitable for beginning students as well as experienced preachers who wish to improve their styles. I encourage everyone to read it cover-to-cover for maximum benefit.

That being said, some preachers will want to get right into the thick of things, and I have designed the book to help you do that.

The opening "Overview: In A Nutshell" will give you a brief outline of the process, and also tell you where to find a more detailed look at specific topics. Each chapter will have its own "Nutshell" as well, so you can see right from the start what skills you will be working on. Along the way, "Hints And Tips" will give you a pithy phrase or sentence that summarizes the essential steps (an appendix lists all the hints and tips). For those who need tangible examples, sample sermons are included, along with introductions that place them in context. Finally, for the really impatient, you can skip to the end of the book to find "The Secret Of Preaching Without A Net." I hope that this arrangement will give maximum instruction to those who need it, while allowing those who do not need the review to skip easily ahead.

This book is dedicated to three preachers who helped develop the content of this book, whether they realize it or not. Mac, Fred, and John: thanks for being there. Thanks also to Stan Purdum, Joyce Scales, Lois Sadler, and Nancy Shepherd for their comments and suggestions.

The question I am asked most often about my preaching is: "How do you do that?" That is, "How do you get up there without any notes and preach those word-perfect, extemporaneous sermons, as if it were the most natural thing in the world?" The answer is that I don't — behind the seemingly spontaneous style is a lot of hard work. But there is no real secret about how I do it; the answer is in this book. The steps between here and there are mostly a matter of common sense. My hope is that with a little practice, one day they will be asking you too, "How do you do that?"

Overview: In A Nutshell

Preaching without a net involves the mastery of the five acts of traditional rhetoric (*see* Chapter 1, "Introduction"):

Invention
Arrangement
Style
Memory
Delivery

Of these, *memory* is the pivotal act around which all the others revolve; if you cannot remember what you want to say, you will never be able to preach without manuscripts or detailed notes. Fortunately, careful attention to the other four acts of rhetoric will help develop your capacity for memory.

Invention helps memory by making your subject matter familiar. I recommend a specific process that will make your weekly subject matter — the Scriptures chosen for the week, and their intersection with modern life — *over*-familiar, so you will be speaking from an abundance of knowledge (*see* Chapter 2, "Study").

Arrangement is also a memory aid. Attention to sermon structure will help the preacher remember what is supposed to be said.

Style or language is also of crucial importance to memory, since words written to be spoken sound different from words meant to be read off the page. An oral rather than a written-sounding style not only helps the preacher's memory, but makes it easier on the hearers (if it is memorable for them, chances are you will be able to remember it too!). To help preachers cultivate an oral style, I recommend a way of writing sermon manuscripts that emphasizes orality and memory (*see* Chapter 3, "Compose").

Memory is of course deeply entwined with *Delivery*. I recommend a specific process of revision and rehearsal, in which the preacher is putting the finishing touches on the oral manuscript in the process of learning the lines by heart. This is not rote memorization, but a dynamic process of interaction between manuscript and memory — the control provided by the manuscript versus the freedom needed to preach without a net. As with the process of study, the goal is to be over-prepared, and speak with confidence, knowing exactly what you want to say and how to say it (*see* Chapter 4, "Stand And Speak").

Some people learn better by example, so I have included several sample sermons with introductions, each dealing with a specific aspect of the sermon process (*see* Chapter 5, "Sample Sermon Manuscripts").

For those of you who can't wait, I've included a one-page summary at the end, "The Secret Of Preaching Without A Net." Feel free to share the secret.

Keep in mind that we are talking about a *process* that leads toward making you comfortable preaching without notes; you don't have to dive in without your manuscript next Sunday. Along the way, I'll show you some baby steps that you can take in order to make the learning curve easier. I'll also be giving you "Hints and Tips" that will summarize key actions crucial to preaching in the paperless pulpit.

Introduction

In a nutshell: Sermons are meant to be spoken, and both form and content follow from this one fact. The ancient rhetorical theory of Cicero, baptized by Augustine, can help us preach in a spontaneous-sounding style by focusing on the five acts of rhetoric: invention, arrangement, style, memory, and delivery.

"What is worse, a sermon that is shallow, or a sermon that is boring?" I frequently pose this question to groups of preachers, and not just to watch them squirm. It goes to the heart of a basic decision we must make about our preaching.

We have all sat through sermons that have danced and played and tripped over matters dear to our hearts without the slightest hint that the preacher knew or even cared that this issue was anything other than an excuse to trot out a display of wordplay or the cutest story from *Pepto-Bismol for the Soul*. The communication is clear enough, perhaps even interesting. But there is no there there. The content is not worthy of our time, let alone our worship space. It skims frivolously over God and humanity, over life and death. It is cotton candy where meat and potatoes should have been on the menu. Whether the sermon is nothing but hollow eloquence, full of sound and wind but signifying nothing, or merely an excuse to wash in the bubblebath of sentimentality, the shallow sermon (what a friend once called "Sermon Lite") leaves the listener feeling frustrated, demeaned, perhaps insulted and downright cheated.

Is Sermon Lite better or worse than listening to an incomprehensible monotone that leaves not only the entire congregation, but even the preacher, tired and numb? Again, we have all sat through the boring sermon. The content is good enough — sound, well-researched, perhaps even profound. But it is stultifying. Either it is encased in jargon that only a seminary professor could love, or it is entangled in tortured syntax that not even an English professor could unwind. It is read off the page in an expressionless monotone, the words like dying insects that flap one wing before falling in a heap in front of the pulpit. If the preacher ever looks up over the rim of his reading specs, it is only to check with embarrassment the clock on the balcony. There is no danger in this pulpit of either sentimentality or alliteration (Lord save us from the sermon that is both shallow and boring!) — there is only hope that it will be over soon, and we can all go to lunch.

When I pose this dilemma in public, it doesn't take long for a group of preachers to conclude that neither shallow nor boring is desirable, that a sermon should be both deep and interesting. This usually leads us into a discussion of the distinction between content and form — between what we say, and how we say it. What we say — our content — is a matter of study, research, and deep thought. How we say it — our form — is another matter entirely. While the content

> The great communicators are those who manage both form and content well; they have something worthwhile to say, and they say it well.

itself may or may not be interesting to us, depending on the subject matter (I for one am not usually interested in the eating habits of snails), any subject may be made interesting by attention to form (I greatly enjoyed the science writing of the late Stephen Jay Gould, who made snail cuisine enticing). Certainly content must have some, well, content, in order to be interesting, but deep content does not ensure attention. How we say those thoughts may make all the difference in whether they are heard. The great communicators are those who manage both form and content well; they have something worthwhile to say, and they say it well. Deep or shallow is a matter of content; interesting or boring, mostly a matter of form.

If I were to press my opening question, however, and make you decide which was worse, boring or shallow, what would you say? I myself have gone through an evolution on this question. For years I believed with Kierkegaard that boredom was the root of all evil. My experience of listening to sermons was primarily an experience of boredom, and it seemed to me nothing could hurt the gospel more than to make it background music for naptime. Then I was forced to sit for some time under a pulpit that radiated a shallow eloquence. Sugar souffle makes for a fine dessert, but a constant diet of it quickly turns the stomach. Good news dies no quicker death than when it is turned into tabloid news. I came to the conclusion that shallow was much more harmful to the pulpit than boring.

Part of the reason I think that shallow is the more harmful of the two is that I don't have a good answer to it, except to tell the preacher to put more time into study. But I doubt that this is a universal cure, because part of the problem with shallow preaching is that it is a matter of taste, and taste cannot be taught. The preacher who indulges in verbal kitsch will not acquire a taste for fine art in the latest Bible commentary — indeed, such a preacher may come away from the commentary with an increased taste for technical jargon and turgid syntax that will mix poorly with a low-brow style.

For those wondering how to make their sermons more interesting, I have more to say. In my years of teaching preaching and listening to sermons both by students and experienced preachers, I have usually heard good and thoughtful content (the shallow preacher really is the rare exception). Most preachers are conscientious — they do their homework, think about what is appropriate to say in the context, and write clear sentences in their sermon manuscripts. The problem is not with their message, but with keeping people interested. To some extent this is a matter of form, but often the real problem with both sermon form and content is delivery.

> The key to preaching that is both thoughtful and interesting is delivery. Delivery determines the sermon.

"What did you think of the sermon?" asks the preacher. "You read it," goes the old reply, "and you read it poorly." The sad truth is that neither thoughtful content nor sparkling form can make a poorly-delivered sermon come to life. This is particularly true of the sermon that is no more than a manuscript read aloud. The boredom here comes from the ear's inability to take in what was meant for the eye. Written communication is qualitatively different from verbal communication; the reader has many opportunities that the listener does not — to go back over a bit of fuzzy syntax and parse it out, to read and re-read a complicated sentence, to look up a word in the dictionary, to flip the page back to remind oneself what the subject was, to take just a few examples. By contrast, the listener who so much as pauses to ponder the meaning of a word may wake up a few seconds or minutes later to find that the entire presentation has passed by. The problem of listening to what should be looked at is complicated when the preacher orates that which should be observed; inevitably, the reading of writing is done in a certain monotone, the words spaced evenly like the fixed-space type of an old typewriter, the sentences punctuated by a predictable pattern of vocal inflection. Such manuscript preaching lacks spontaneity; it sounds rote. It is hard to mistake the sound of someone reading something off a page. It is also hard to listen to for very long, unless the reader is particularly skilled at reading. This is why acting is best left to professionals.

Actors and preachers have this in common: their words are meant from the beginning to be uttered in public, not read in private. The playwright conceives a play from the beginning as an event — something that can be embodied in space and time, with real people on the stage and in the audience. The play is never merely the words on the page of the script; the playwright knows this from the beginning, and it determines how the words go down on the page. Should it be any different for the preacher? In our case, of course, the playwright will also be the actor, and this is crucial to the process. We write with delivery in mind.

In preaching, delivery determines form and content. We preachers know from the beginning that we are not just putting words down on the page. We are going to be preaching to a particular congregation, standing in a particular pulpit. We can visualize the space — the pews, the carpet, the hangings, the faces of those who sit in the same places week after week. Our preaching is from the very beginning embodied in that time and place. The sermon is not the words we put down on paper, any more than a play is simply a script. Once we understand that the sermon is what happens there — what is delivered in that church, that Sunday, to those people — then we are on our way to understanding how to go about preparing for that moment.

The key to preaching that is both thoughtful and interesting is delivery. Delivery determines the sermon — but not in the sense that all a preacher need do is cultivate a new way of putting across the same old stuff, as if hyperventilated Sunday morning antics could breathe life into a dead sermon manuscript. Sermon delivery determines every aspect of the sermon process in the deepest sense, once we realize that the ultimate goal of the preaching process is what happens on Sunday morning, and everything we do to prepare for that moment, involving both form and content, is governed by our ultimate purpose. We are going to deliver a sermon; that is what we are called to do. Our function is to preach, and that means to speak. Form and content follow function.

> The most basic decision every preacher must make is whether to allow the nature of the sermon as an oral, communal event to have its full impact on the entire process of sermon production and delivery.

The most basic decision every preacher must make is whether to allow the nature of the sermon as an oral, communal event to have its full impact on the entire process of sermon production and delivery. If sermons are meant to be read off a page, then by all means read away — and run the risk of boring your congregation to tears. If, however, what you mean by "the sermon" is what is going to happen when you open your mouth on Sunday morning, then the written page will begin to play a subservient role in your preaching. Gradually, you will come to understand the various functions words on a page play in the ultimate production of the sermon. Paper will play a less important role in the sermon, because the sermon is words in time and space, not words on paper. Eventually, you will wean yourself from pulpit paper entirely. No longer will you be bound by the chain of a manuscript; you will be free to speak to the people. No paper will get in your way. You won't even miss the paper, let alone feel insecure or tongue-tied — you won't need the wood-pulp security blanket any longer. The paper is not the sermon; your words are. You will be preaching without a net, and liking it.

The ancient Roman poet Horace (65-8 B.C.) once said that the purpose of his writing was to "profit with delight": "He gains every vote who mingles profit with delight by pleasing and instructing the reader at the same time" (*Ars Poetica,* 343). "To profit with delight" is also a good motto for the preacher who wishes to work without a net, and deliver both thoughtful and interesting content. Profit involves content; delight results from form; both flow from the fact of delivery. For a deeper understanding of how the end result — sermon delivery — influences the entire process of sermon study and composition, we now turn to the education of Horace and his contemporaries, and its legacy for Christian preaching, both ancient and modern.

Rhetoric To The Rescue

Horace was not taught to write poetry; he was taught to make speeches. For those of us raised on a school curriculum of reading, writing, and arithmetic, it may be hard to imagine a school system based on public speaking, but that was precisely the way the Romans taught their children how to read and write. They taught them rhetoric.

Roman children like Horace (and the Apostle Paul, along perhaps with other New Testament authors) were taught to read and write from rhetorical handbooks. These handbooks consisted of graded exercises that covered the necessary skills of oratory. The handbooks broke down the complicated rules of public speaking into bite-sized parts, each of which became the basis of practice, drill, and repetition for young schoolboys (women were not generally admitted to rhetorical education). At the elementary level, the training covered grammar, moving from easy rhetorical figures to more difficult, each exercise building on the previous, until the student was able to complete first a written thesis, then an actual speech. After completing elementary studies, the student could move to an advanced school of rhetoric, where the details of rhetorical theory were taught. The rhetorical curriculum, systematized and standardized, held sway in education for several hundred years.

The classic Greco-Roman rhetorical tradition was definitively summarized in the first century before Christ by Horace's older contemporary, Cicero (106-43 B.C.). In seven masterful works on rhetoric, Cicero drew upon the tradition that had been handed down to him, summing up while moving forward in a significant way. We cannot begin to do justice to the complexities of Cicero's work here (those Roman schoolboys spent

> **Cicero taught the five acts of rhetoric:**
> *Invention*
> *Arrangement*
> *Style*
> *Memory*
> *Delivery*

years trying to master it), nor do we need to. But we can gain some insight into modern public speaking — in our case, preaching, to be particular — through the master of ancient Roman rhetoric.

Cicero, like those before him, thought of rhetoric as consisting of five acts. Each of these acts was vital to the final product; none could be ignored without peril to the whole. But each was a separate and distinct act — none could be folded into one of the others without losing something crucial. It was important for the orator to pay attention to each of the five acts individually, giving them all their proper weight. The five acts of rhetoric were:

Invention
Arrangement
Style
Memory
Delivery

Invention (Latin *inventio*) was the process of coming up with something to say; it involved content. Invention was research or study. The Latin word *inventio* meant "to come upon" or "find"; it was roughly equivalent to the Greek word preserved in our expression, "Eureka!" (which originally meant "I found it!"). The process of invention led to the Eureka moment, when the speaker came across the heart of the content of the speech. But the entire process of research or study provided the raw materials for the speech as a whole. Here the rhetorician was simply interested in all that could be discovered about the subject at hand. In the immortal words of Sgt. Joe Friday, invention was "Just the facts, ma'am."

Arrangement (*dispositio*) was just what it seems to be: the ordering of facts into the various parts of the speech. Arrangement involved form in the sense of structure. In the Roman rhetorical tradition, every speech had a set number of parts and a set order; every speech was basically the same in terms of its structure. Each speech had six main parts: the Introduction (*exordium*), designed to win the speaker favorable attention; the Statement or Narration (*narratio*) of the case; the Partition or Division (*partitio* or *divisio*) of the case, which announced the various headings under which the case was to be discussed; the Proofs or Confirmation (*confirmatio*) or constructive arguments; the Refutation (*refutatio*) of the claims of opponents; and finally the Summary (*peroratio*) which included a final appeal. As is obvious from this structure, Roman oratory was geared practically toward the political and legal sphere, yet this structure for public speaking was quite influential, even in Christian preaching, for hundreds of years. I dare say you could detect it at work today.

Style (*elocutio*) involved language. Style was another aspect of form; it was the choice of words used by the speaker. For Cicero and the Roman rhetoricians, style was to have four virtues: clarity, correctness, appropriateness, and embellishment. Clarity, of course, was and is the virtue without which there can be no communication at all. Correctness was a matter of the grammar taught at the elementary level. Appropriateness was judged according to the function of the language: was this particular section intended to inform the audience, to please them, or to persuade them? Cicero spoke of these three different functions as the "plain," "middle," and "grand" styles — respectively for information, pleasure, and persuasion (thus Cicero agreed with Horace that a speech should teach and delight, but he added another purpose — to persuade, to move the will). Embellishment involved "figures of thought" (language that was used to emphasize one's points, like the rhetorical question) and "figures of language" (verbal patterns like parallelism, antithesis, and climax).

Memory (*memoria*) was essential to the Roman orator. Whether one wrote out the speech *in toto,* or spoke extemporaneously (both methods were used), one simply did not speak unless one was prepared to do so without written notes. You didn't even get to use an outline or a crib sheet; if you could not remember it, you did not say it. Memory involved both the order of one's arguments and substance of each proof. Mind you, the Romans did not stand up in court or the public square without a few memory tricks up their sleeve; part of the rhetorical training involved learning *how* to use one's memory. For example, orators used visual association in order to remember the order of argument; they pictured the parts of the speech as rooms in a house, and visualized themselves walking through the house as they moved from one part to the other.

Delivery (*actio*) was the final act of rhetoric. It was also the most crucial, being the culmination of all the other acts — the whole point was to give a speech. I am happy to say that Cicero agreed with me: "Delivery is the single dominant power in oratory," he said (*De Oratore,* 3.213). Due to the importance of delivery, the rhetorical handbooks contained myriad rules and regulations regarding the proclamation of a speech. Nothing about delivery was left to chance. The rules about delivery covered not only the act of moving your mouth to make the words themselves, but every bodily movement involved in speech-making, including facial expression and nonverbal movement. Delivery was everything.

This has not been merely a history lesson. The Roman rhetorical tradition was designed to teach speakers to do exactly the kind of thing we want to do: speak clearly, beautifully, and apparently off-the-cuff. Those who would preach without a net can learn much from Cicero's division of the act of speaking into five acts — in particular, we will need to pay attention to the now-neglected fourth act, *memoria*.

> The Roman rhetorical tradition was designed to teach speakers to do exactly the kind of thing we want to do: speak clearly, beautifully, and apparently off-the-cuff.

But before we move to the practical lessons that Cicero can give modern preachers, we have to ask whether it is legitimate to draw these lessons from such a source — can we really learn preaching from some dusty treatises on legal and political rhetoric? To put it crassly, is this even Christian? Fortunately for us, the question was answered long ago.

Baptizing Cicero

Like Horace, Paul, and countless other Roman schoolboys, Augustine (354-430 A.D.) was trained to read and write using the rhetorical handbooks. Like Cicero, he received advanced training in rhetoric and became a teacher. But Augustine was haunted by a God who would not leave him and his academic pursuits alone. Attracted by the rhetorical power of the sermons of Ambrose, Augustine surrendered to his pursuer-God and was baptized and ordained, eventually becoming a bishop in the African town of Hippo. He wrote some of the most influential Christian theological works of all time. Included in his extensive body of writings is a handbook on biblical interpretation (*De Doctrina Christiana*, or *On Christian Doctrine*), the final chapter of which is one of the oldest and most influential essays on the art of Christian preaching.

Augustine was himself no slouch when it came to preaching — we still have over one thousand of his sermons in manuscript form! After his conversion to Christianity, he did not totally abandon all that he had learned from Cicero and the great Greco-Roman rhetorical tradition. Instead, the best of Cicero was modified according to a new standard, that of the source of Christian teaching, the Scriptures. Augustine took for granted that Christian preachers would be trained in secular eloquence. There was nothing wrong in that; indeed, a great deal could be learned. Yet all that was learned in the rhetorical handbooks was to take a back seat to what was to be gleaned from Scripture. Cicero was to be immersed in the Bible. In essence, Augustine baptized Cicero.

For Augustine, there were two parts to biblical interpretation: discovery and teaching. Discovery was a matter of the rules of biblical interpretation, and was covered in the first three chapters of *On Christian Doctrine*. Teaching involved preaching, and this was the subject of the final chapter. Since there was no need to rehearse all that could be learned in the secular schools of rhetoric, Augustine gave this advice: learn the rules, but use them freely. Most important for the Christian preacher was to learn how to speak not from the rules but from the Bible, whose eloquence no one

> **Augustine baptized Cicero, immersing rhetorical tradition in biblical tradition.**

could doubt: "With what a river of eloquence they flow even he who snores must notice" (*On Christian Doctrine*, 4.7.12; my quotations are taken from D. W. Robertson's translation).

Augustine agreed with Cicero that the purpose of speaking was to teach, delight, and move. He even quoted Cicero as "a certain eloquent man" who said, " 'To teach is a necessity, to please is a sweetness, to persuade is a victory' " (4.12.27, quoting Cicero, *Orator*, 21.69). However, Augustine gave Cicero's purpose a Christian shading; the purpose of teaching was actually to explain, edify, and convert — to touch the heart, head, and will for God.

In fact, Augustine believed that secular eloquence was secondary to religious content. If you can't speak eloquently, he said, speak wisely (thus giving us his answer to our original question in this chapter — shallow is worse!). Wisdom, for Augustine, came from studying the Scriptures: one "speaks more or less wisely to the extent that he has become more or less proficient in the Holy Scriptures" (4.5.7). The words of Scripture were more important than all the rules of rhetoric, for not only did they contain the wisdom of God, they were a source of natural eloquence: "not only can nothing seem to me more wise than they are, but also nothing can seem more eloquent" (4.6.9). The preacher could thus learn not only content but form directly from the Bible.

Still, Augustine was not one to disparage all that he had learned from Cicero. It was simply a matter of Christian priority. Above all, the message that came from God was to be heard. Clarity was given priority over eloquence: he advised preachers that the figures of rhetoric had their place, "but in all their utterances [preachers] should first of all seek to speak so that they may be understood" (4.8.22). Eloquence for its own sake was to be avoided. "The speaker should not consider the eloquence of his teaching but the clarity of it" (4.9.23). Of primary importance was the message itself, because "instruction should come before persuasion" (4.12.28). "He who teaches should thus avoid all words which do not teach" (4.10.134).

Nevertheless, "delight has no small place in the art of eloquence" (4.13.29). While of the three functions of rhetoric — teaching, pleasing, persuading — the teaching of the Christian faith was primary, still Augustine wanted to persuade the hearers, and eloquence could be no small factor in that kind of conversion. Delight and persuasion were necessary only where there was resistance to the teaching. In such cases, a baptized Cicero could come in quite handy. But in the end, speaking plainly trumped speaking eloquently: "He who cannot do both should say wisely what he cannot say eloquently rather than say eloquently what he says foolishly" (4.28.61).

Augustine applied the lessons of rhetoric not only to the speech but also to the life of the Christian preacher. One should live as an example of the truth one lives by. If one lives well, said Augustine, there may be an eloquence to his life that will convert even those most resistant to rhetoric. "The life of the speaker has greater weight in determining whether he is obediently heard than any grandness of eloquence" (4.27.59).

In short, Augustine established importance of rhetoric, yet freed Christian preaching from dependence on it. Cicero was baptized, but relativized. More important than eloquence was the teaching of Scripture. Eloquence was not disdained or discarded — indeed, one could learn eloquence from the Scripture itself, apart from the rules of Cicero. But one could also easily use Cicero for God's purposes. This is precisely what Augustine did. Many of the rules taught by Cicero went by the wayside — for example, Augustine's daily preaching often consisted of verse-by-verse exposition, rather than the set speech form of Cicero's rhetoric; in contrast to the eloquent conclusions of lawyers and politicians, we sometimes find at the end of a sermon by Augustine, "We're out of time; we'll pick up here tomorrow." But when Cicero could be brought into service, Augustine had no trouble using all the tools at his command.

Augustine's reputation for rhetorical brilliance lived on: the next Bishop of Hippo said of his passing, "Now the cricket chirps, for the swan is silent." However, modern readers may find his language — along with that of Cicero — more stiff than inviting. Even the plain style of Augustine's prose seems rather grand today (particularly in the older translations that are commonly available). I was recently amused to find *On Christian Doctrine* reviewed by an Amazon.com reader who said, "I found this book to be a bit dated" (!).

There is something to be said for what we can learn from a culture and time far removed from our own — as are the Scriptures themselves, we should remember — nevertheless, language, speech, and rhetoric have changed dramatically from the time of

Augustine (and even from the language of more recent times — just read Dickens). I believe that we can learn something important from the rhetoric of Cicero, and Augustine's religious use of it, but we must also be clear about the ways rhetoric has changed in recent years.

Conversational Eloquence

Recently rhetoric has undergone a dramatic change, a change fueled by technology rather than language itself. Rhetoric has been changed by electricity: in particular, amplification and transmission. Amplification has allowed speakers to communicate with quieter voices at louder volumes, and transmission — radio, television, and now computers and multimedia — has set a new standard for how these relatively quiet voices may be eloquent.

The chief change that amplification and transmission have brought about is the movement toward a more conversational style of rhetoric. If you listen to old-time radio, it can sound quite bombastic, as if people were shouting at the microphone. In fact, they were orating, following a traditional style that was designed to fill a large reverberant room in the days before amplification. Only the strongest voices could be heard in the back row, and words were declaimed in a deliberate style, so that each could be heard distinctly. Early film and television acting often had the same overdone quality — necessary for the stage, if the actors were to project to a large audience, but much too much for the close-up camera. What happened, of course, is that actors and speakers quickly learned to adapt, to develop quieter voices before the microphone, and quieter actions before the camera. A whisper could now carry to the back row with the help of an amplifier; a wink could be carried by the camera into our living rooms. As the twentieth century moved along, the standard for eloquence became no longer the distant speaker on a platform declaiming periodic sentences in round tones, but the talk-show host bantering with his genial sidekick. It was Johnny Carson, not William Jennings Bryan. Amplification and transmission had made the preferred standard for rhetoric more conversational.

The move toward a conversational rhetoric had inevitable results for preaching. Even sermons from as late as the 1950s sound over-formal to our ears; amplification had not yet penetrated any but the largest and richest pulpits, and sermons on radio and television retained much of the old rhetorical style that was still at work among newscasters and announcers (the "thees" and "thous" didn't help much either). In the 1960s, church membership declined as people began to see it as too old-fashioned and irrelevant to modern life; preachers and liturgists clung to the old style of rhetoric long past its time, adding to the feeling that the church was out-of-date. When the reaction set in, the church experimented with preaching that threw the old rules to the wind, and parishioners began experiencing interactive sermons and talk-show-style panel discussions — and even more folk left. It is no wonder that the next big change in preaching came with the adoption of "inductive" and "narrative" preaching styles —

> Amplification and transmission have brought about a more conversational style of rhetoric.

which at their heart were more conversational and informal. Amplification — now relatively cheap — became desirable even in smaller churches; and anyone who had the will and some discretionary cash could get on public access cable TV — even more reason to cultivate a TV-friendly style. The standard has clearly changed, as more and more church folk are calling for worship to include multimedia and MTV-style video, while even at the smallest and most traditional churches, people want an amplified pulpit — "So the older folks can hear you," they say, but what they mean is either that they want a more conversational style, or that they really cannot hear the preacher who speaks as if there actually were a microphone (because that is the standard for eloquence these days).

Modern, media-formed people value an off-the-cuff-sounding eloquence, like that of the club comedian or talk-show host. It is a different style of eloquence from that of Cicero, Augustine, and the great preachers and orators of the past; it is plain, not grand. It seeks to persuade by subtlety and innuendo rather than bombast. It does not require listeners to follow long, complicated sentence structure, nor does it take delight in the perfectly balanced periodic clauses of old. At its wittiest, it values the snappy comeback. At its crassest, it exalts the soundbite.

The great irony of modern education is that as oral style was undergoing a great change due to technology, the study of rhetoric fell into neglect. No longer were school children taught using handbooks of rhetoric; rather, they were taught to value written communication, to read silently and not aloud, to write and not to speak. Speech communication was an option in high school and college, rarely a requirement. Training in mass media communication — requiring expensive equipment — was restricted to professionals and their apprentices. Oral training was neglected in favor of writing. Perhaps recent years have brought some change with the proliferation of relatively inexpensive media technology and the advent of computer multimedia, but there is little emphasis on orality per se — the assumption is that we are going to make a video, not stand in front of a group of real live people and speak (what, without even a PowerPoint slide show?). The result is that preachers in training today — even those with media backgrounds — are well-prepared to write something, film something, or record something — but perhaps not quite ready to stand in the pulpit of their first small congregation (where there is still no microphone, but maybe we can get it into the budget next year) and deliver a sermon.

Should we just give up and start rolling the overhead projectors and the multimedia screens into the sanctuary? Before we throw the church budget into a coma, we should consider the signs that oral communication — perhaps unamplified, definitely transmitted only by line-of-sight — is alive and well and necessary. Corporations still pay consultants to train their executives to speak well in public, whether the camera is present or not. Politicians and lawyers are still called to make their cases before real live people, as well as the camera. And even in the media, a single speaker on the radio can be riveting for hours; a pair having a conversation can keep a movie audience interested, even with no action. Just talking can keep people entertained for hours; all across the country, conversation is alive. The spoken word has still a certain compelling power. Preachers do not need multimedia (nor even microphones); they can be spellbinding simply on the force of their language. Do we need a multimedia church in this new age? Perhaps. But perhaps for preachers the answer is a more integrated oral and visual style — or an oral style that incorporates visuality (I'll have more to say about this later).

Modern electronic media and amplification have definitely changed our cultural standards of eloquence, but before we jump to the (still somewhat expensive) panacea of the video church, we need to cultivate a more oral approach to preaching. Modern preaching has placed entirely too much emphasis on writing — we speak of "writing a sermon," we take our sermon manuscripts into the pulpit and read them, we vote on the Ten Greatest Preachers in the World based on their publications, when most of us have never heard these people deliver a sermon. Even our best sermon textbooks emphasize Cicero's first three acts of rhetoric — Invention, Arrangement, and Style — at the expense of Memory and Delivery. Preaching books speak of how to study the Bible and make relevant connections to the congregation, how to organize the sermon, and how to put it in appropriate language — dozens or hundreds of pages on the topic of form and content — but then they conclude with a handful of pages about delivery, which Cicero called the "single dominant power" of rhetoric!

A key element of classical rhetoric has been almost totally ignored in modern preaching: *memoria*. After all, who needs it? The television announcer has the TelePrompTer; the radio newscaster has ticker-tape notes. The preacher in the pulpit has a manuscript, or notes. But who has not been embarrassed to listen to the announcer reading nonsensical or ungrammatical cues, or the preacher who loses the place in the manuscript or cannot decipher the notes? At least the announcer is reading someone else's copy (and has someone else to blame) — but the preacher at least ought to know what is to be said. Is this not an instance where we can learn from both ancient and modern rhetoric — what is more natural than to remember something that was designed for the way we normally speak, a conversational style?

For the preacher who wishes to work without a net, Cicero's fourth act of rhetoric is the crucial hinge on which the whole sermon process will swing. If the final act of rhetoric, delivery, is the culmination of preaching, the next-to-last, memory, will determine how effective that culmination will be. Memory must be kept in mind from the beginning to the end of the process. It will govern our study and our composition, the arrangement of sections and the choice of words, the illustrations and examples, and of course the actual words that come out of our mouths on Sunday morning. Without memory, sermon study is merely academic, sermon composition an essay exercise, and delivery a needlessly painful experience for all. With memory, the other acts will flow together as one.

> Modern preaching has placed too much emphasis on writing and neglected the role of memory.

The key to developing a more spontaneous preaching style is *sounding* off-the-cuff, without actually *being* off-the-cuff. Take a cue from the talk-show host or stand-up comic — these people are *actors*. They are not just doing what comes naturally, but have rehearsed and honed and practiced. Their talent is their ability to make it sound easy and natural. But they are highly prepared. And they rely heavily on memory.

This is not to say that writing is not a helpful tool in preaching. The preacher will write throughout the process — research notes, brainstorming notes, outlines, drafts in various states of revision. There will be many pieces of paper, each in its place. The preacher's five acts of rhetoric all involve different uses of paper. But the goal is to speak — the sermon is what happens on Sunday morning, not what you put down on a piece of paper. If you are going to preach without a net, you are going to wean yourself away from relying on paper in the final and culminating act of the sermon, which is delivery, the sermon itself. Those pieces of paper are not the sermon. Some of that paper you will file on Sunday afternoon; consider that paper the written detritus of what was once a sermon. But you can never file away the sermon, which is an event in space and time, not something written on a page. The pulpit is paperless.

We wish to sound natural when we preach. That means we will take on a conversational style. That means we will *not* be reading a sermon from notes. We *will* be talking to the people, with no pieces of paper between us and them. We will *not* talk off-the-cuff. We will *sound* off-the-cuff. Our goal is to develop a spontaneous-sounding style, and that will take practice. We will develop our memory in order to give the most effective delivery.

The plan of this book follows the ancient acts of rhetoric: first we will consider what it means to study (Cicero's *invention*), then to compose (*arrangement* and *style*), and finally, to stand and speak (*memory* and *delivery*). We want to learn a paperless preaching style, but we cannot speak of memory and delivery without first dealing with issues of form and content. Every act of the preaching process leads to and is governed by the final act, the actual delivery of the sermon (we will refer to this act, and only this act, as "the sermon"; all the other acts are simply part of the sermon process). By keeping in mind the final act throughout the process, we can learn to study and compose for the most rhetorically effective, spontaneous-sounding delivery, i.e., we can learn to preach without a net.

Our goal is delivery; our purpose is to "profit with delight" — to inform a congregation, interest them, and spark their will toward God. But we will always keep in mind Augustine's emphasis on the priority of the message. We'll interest them if we can, persuade them if we are able — but our main job is to be faithful bearers of the message. Technique is not a means in and of itself, but is offered to God. Our goal is to speak good news about God in the grace of Jesus Christ. We are not going to indulge in phony memory tricks, rhetorical games to fool a congregation into thinking they have heard something, because phony simply will not do. There must be emotional congruence between preacher and message in order to preach without a net; it cannot be done with content the preacher does not believe — that the preacher does not live by. "One who is not himself first a hearer in his inner being will be only a hollow preacher," said Augustine. "Whether one is just now making ready to speak before the people or before any other group or is composing something to be spoken later before the people or to be read by those who wish to do so or are able to do so, he should pray that God may place a good speech in his mouth" (*On Christian Doctrine*, 4.30.63). Again, this prayer is not a hollow act nor a formal show. We speak as we live. The most important thing we can do to learn to preach without a net is to live as people whose only net is God.

Study

In a nutshell: Preaching in the paperless pulpit requires study to the extent that you are over-prepared to preach. Study life and Scripture and their intersection, because preaching is a reading of Scripture to and for a particular audience. Good study habits will enhance your ongoing process of preparation; I suggest one such study system here.

The preacher who would work without a net, like all preachers, will need to pay attention to the acts of classical rhetoric: study (Cicero's *invention*), composition (*arrangement* and *style*), and speaking (*memory* and *delivery*). Like all preachers, we must consider the final act, delivery, to be the goal and culmination of the process — our purpose is to speak, and so delivery is the light at the end of the tunnel. But if we wish to preach in a more spontaneous style, then it is not just delivery but *memory* that sheds light on the other acts of sermon creation. Or to mix the metaphor, everything that goes through the sieve of delivery must first go through the funnel of memory. That which cannot be remembered cannot be delivered.

Mind you, we are not talking about the dry, dusty process of rote memory. Our goal is to develop a spontaneous, conversational style of sermon, not to memorize words that are neither spontaneous nor conversational. I am not suggesting that you write up your sermon manuscript in the usual way, then spend hours committing every last dry morsel to memory. That will not turn your manuscript sermon into a vital piece of spontaneous communication. It will probably make it even drier, and may subject your congregation to what one homiletician has described as the painful experience of watching you "read your manuscript off the backs of your eyeballs," perhaps stumbling, perhaps apologizing, perhaps twitching in forgetful agony. This is the exact opposite of the preaching style we wish to learn!

To understand the role of memory in the sermon process is to realize that what cannot be remembered *should not* be delivered. The old manuscript cannot be preached from memory, because it was not memorable to begin with. It was meant not for memory, but for reading. At best, it is a first draft for the sermon without a net. If we are truly going to preach without a net, we must from the beginning take memory into account. The entire sermon process is guided by delivery, and delivery is governed by memory, therefore everything must first pass the test of memory. We begin, continue, and end with memory in mind.

This is perhaps the time for reassurance: what I will be asking you to do is far from impossible — quite the opposite, for by the time you have finished this book and implemented its procedures, this kind of preaching will seem the most natural way of doing things. Let me repeat: you will *not* be required to memorize your present written manuscripts by rote. Our goal rather is to rethink the entire sermon process with memory in mind; the sermon manuscripts you will begin to write will be of another order entirely, because they will be written to be said rather than read. What you put down on the page will be meant to be remembered from the beginning, and this is what makes preaching without a net possible — and desirable, for after all, if *you* can't remember it, how can you expect anyone else to remember it?

> What cannot be remembered should not be delivered. Begin, continue, and end with memory in mind.

Another note of reassurance for the manuscript preacher who wishes to begin working without a net: we don't take the net away immediately. We are talking about a *process* of weaning ourselves away from paper in the pulpit, which begins by looking at paper in a whole new way. We do not simply abandon our manuscripts and walk into the pulpit unprepared — a sure prescription for disaster. We aren't even going to ban paper from the pulpit, as if not having notes or outlines or manuscripts would magically make us eloquent where we were not before. There is nothing magical in the process, nor anything wrong with having in the pulpit whatever you need to help you preach. The paperless pulpit is a method, a way of working. Our goal is simply to develop a style that relies less on paper in the pulpit, because it is geared to speaking, not reading. It will not happen overnight, and there may be baby steps as we move along — one day we will take a manuscript into the pulpit and turn the pages but rarely refer to it, another day we may take only an outline or notes or a listing of the first lines of each section, until the day when we take no paper with us and truly preach without a net. I don't expect you to do the high-wire act on your first day of training; it took me seven years of preaching before I figured out how to do it, and was able to stand and speak confidently without a manuscript, and then only after sitting for some time under a preacher who was a skilled model of the spontaneous, conversational-sounding style.

The usual objection to an expanded role for memory in preaching is that it takes too much time. "We're busy pastors," we say. "We don't have time to *memorize* things!" Again, the objection is based on the false supposition of rote memory — we are not talking about merely memorizing the same old sermon manuscripts, but of coming with a new kind of manuscript that lends itself to memory. It is much easier to learn something that was meant to be learned (thus a novel must be put into the form of a screenplay before the actors tackle it). And if it was not meant

> Allow one hour of preparation, including study, rehearsal, and revision, for every minute you plan to speak.

to be learned, why would we inflict it on our congregations? The time required for the additional step of memory is not as great as one might think, because the road we will travel is not the steep one that goes directly up the face of the mountain before us, but the easier one off to the side — the mountain is conquered in more manageable steps. The objection is on target only for those looking for a shortcut — a way of avoiding work on the sermon. Some people may be fooled by the seeming ease of the actor into believing that there is no script to be learned, that it is all improvisation. I have nothing to offer such preachers here, for the simple reason that there is no shortcut. The method I am proposing is intended as a way of improving the quality of your preaching, which simply cannot be done without practice. A good sermon takes more time in preparation than a bad one. I subscribe to the old rule of thumb, that the sermon requires an hour of preparation for every minute of preaching; following this method, the preacher should expect to spend ten to fifteen hours during the week preparing for the typical ten-to-fifteen minute Sunday sermon (about half of that time will be spent in study, the other half in composition and revision/rehearsal). Of course, some weeks the sermon comes more easily than others, and we will look at ways experienced preachers can lessen their load by working smarter. But preaching successfully without a net is not a time-saver; we do not go into the pulpit less prepared but more prepared than the old-fashioned manuscript preacher. As someone once put it, the speeches that require the most rehearsal are the extemporaneous ones!

So we begin at the beginning, with study. But in every act of study, we realize that the ultimate goal is delivery, and that the kind of spontaneous, off-the-cuff preaching style we are seeking requires a delivery funneled through memory. Our study from the beginning will seek that which is memorable, simply because it must.

Life

The preacher who rushes to the commentaries and sermon helps in anticipation of Sunday has started in the wrong place. Scripture study is indeed essential to the sermon; the Bible is the source of the good news and the basic bibliography of the Christian faith.

But every act of communication begins with a purpose: we intend to communicate such-and-such. And every purpose requires an audience: we will communicate such-and-such to so-and-so. There can be no act of communication without an audience, and thus no content stands independent of its hearers. Much has been written about the influence of audiences upon meaning, some of it hyperbole, but there is no doubt that the picture one has in mind while doing things with words affects how those words come out in the end.

Let me give you one example. The story goes that an Oxford don was called to fill in one Sunday at an old country church. The Old Testament reading was a long and dry passage from one of the historical works concerning a king of Israel. The aged professor got into the pulpit, looked out over the congregation of farmers, laborers, and assorted rustics, and said, "You may think that we are speaking of Jeroboam I, but actually, it's Jeroboam II." What sort of act of communication is that? It is perfectly comprehensible in the Oxford seminar room, but here it leaves the assorted rustics, laborers, and farmers scratching their heads — they did not even know there was more than one Jeroboam. It is tempting to say that no act of communication has taken place, but that would be incorrect, for the scholar has communicated much more than he intended — his misunderstanding of his congregation. He made the mistake of starting his study with the Scriptures, which he never left long enough to consider his intended audience.

As we shall see, it is quite a mistake to assume even the basics of Scriptural knowledge among our listeners — even those who know the story will need to be prodded and reminded on occasion — and an even greater mistake to use the technical language of biblical studies in our sermons. It is not that technical terms are bad — they are simply technical. Everyone has a language that they use in work; lawyers speak legalese, doctors use medical jargon, computer programmers speak C++ or Java. We use technical language because it is a shortcut — it communicates quickly and concisely to others who know the language. But think of how long it takes to learn a technical language — years of seminary, law school, medical school. It is not our intention to teach our congregations to be professional biblical scholars (and even if it were, we could not accomplish much in an hour per week). We seek rather to proclaim the good news about God's grace in Jesus Christ. Since our audience is not a technical one, we will not speak in technical terms. We have learned the technical terms ourselves in order to do the greatest justice to our study: we can easily handle commentaries, concordances, and other tools.

> Our audience determines what we say and how we say it. We wish to proclaim good news, so our study begins with the lives of those who would hear that news.

We have been trained to do it, so that others do not have to — just as we rely on lawyers to do legal work, doctors to do medical work, and computer programmers to keep our machines running, so we preachers study the Bible in ways the average member of our congregations cannot. This is not elitism, but a simple recognition of our function; it would be elitism to assume that everyone should communicate on our level of expertise, simply because we can.

So our audience determines what we say and how we say it. This is as it should be. We don't expect our lawyer to lecture the jury on case precedents; the jury is not the judge, and requires persuasion, not legalese. We want our doctor to give us an explanation of why it hurts; we don't appreciate an explanation shrouded in medical terms we do not understand. We turn on our computers and expect the software to work; if the screen turns blue and gives us a series of incomprehensible numbers, we do not thank the programmer, but turn the machine off and start again, hoping we won't have to call technical support today. If we do call technical support, we expect to be told how to get the thing to work; we don't want to hear about object-oriented programming in an enterprise environment, whatever that may be.

In our case, we wish to proclaim good news to a people in need of hearing that news, and so our study will begin not with the good news itself, but the lives of those who would hear that news. Who are these people whose lives we study? To some extent we know, because we see many of them week after week, sitting in the same pews. To some extent we do not know, however, because we see them only for that hour and perhaps a few more — they have 167 more hours to live each week, where we see only dimly — and besides, they are not the only ones who sit in our pews and need to hear the news. Sometimes strangers disrupt the orderly predictability of this or that pew for a week or two — what will we say to them? Our study must take the broadest focus possible. We must study Life.

The first step in studying Life is simply to live it. Grow up, go to school, get a job, have a family. Be a person. Wake up and smell the media. Books, film, radio, television, magazines, web pages, music. Have a conversation with a small child every now and then. Have a confrontation with a teenager. Visit the elderly in a nursing home. Travel. When in doubt, talk to people. No hermit can preach. To convey the good news effectively into a particular situation requires that one be immersed in that particular situation; you cannot be cut off from humanity and speak to that same humanity — thus God became human. Preachers, too, must be human. One who would study Life must first be engaged fully with it.

The next step in studying Life is to observe it. How many times have you been introduced to someone and five minutes later realize that you have no idea what that person's name is? It happens to me all the time — at first I thought it was simply because I had a bad memory for names, but then I realized that most times, I was not paying enough attention at the time I heard the name, and so I never really heard it at all. Life so easily slips by, and the preacher will take care not only to live it but also to observe it. What is that person opposite you on the train wearing? Color of hair, eyes, shape of ear? I take this walk every day — could I go home and write a detailed description of the path and the sights along the way? To observe is not merely to pay attention, but to use the imagination to reconstruct Life. The same applies to all our pursuits; to study Life is to observe it keenly, not merely thumbing through the pages, noting the headlines and ads, but to stop every now and then and engage the story wholly.

Most of all, to study Life is to cultivate a genuine interest in other people. Being interested in people is the secret to success in preaching as well as pastoring. I remember a colleague in my early days of ministry speaking of a man in his church: "I'd like to get him to consider ordination. He'd make a great pastor. He loves people. That's the main thing you need. You have to love people." The study of Life that springs from the love of people will make all the difference in how you are heard on Sunday. People are not interested in how clever you are, how well you string words together, or how much you know about the Bible. They are interested in themselves. That is the first shell you have to crack on Sunday morning. You can't do it without genuine interest in people. You can't do it without the study of Life. To be technically proficient in the acts of rhetoric, but to hate people, is as if the musician were technically perfect but tone deaf. The music is accurate, but lifeless.

We do not study Life merely to cultivate our common humanity. Life also embodies our message. Life is the gospel, worked out over and over again. This is the message of the Incarnation, that God's work is embedded in this world: life imitates gospel. As human beings are created in the image of God, so our encounters with each other can be to some small degree a reflection of that God. The mother scrimps and saves from two jobs to send her son to college. A father takes an errant and disobedient daughter into his arms. A stranger stops to give a hand to someone who has fallen in the street. Are not all these parables of the kingdom, instances of God's good news in miniature? Every time the church acts as if it were the Church, the gospel is proclaimed. The gospel is not mere words in a dusty old scroll — it lives, breathes, pulsates in our midst. If we open our eyes, we can see the myriad ways God's story is recapitulated in this world. At such a moment, our study may turn into prayer. The Holy Spirit is among us; hush, for this is holy ground.

In observing Life, we are not necessarily looking for sermon examples and illustrations, but we will keep an eye out for that which is *memorable*. Those things that are directly useful in our sermon composition are limited to material that is easily remembered, and worth remembering. We are going to be preaching without a net, and thus relying on our own memories; it is easier to start with material that is itself memorable. Moreover, because it is memorable, it is more appropriate to the sermon, because our hearers will be able to remember it as well. There is the story about the old preacher who counted up the sermons he had preached to his congregation — umpteen thousand some-hundred, he discovered, and nobody could remember a single one of them! But if the preacher had started with material that was memorable to begin with, the story would have been different. If we use examples and illustrations from Life that are easily remembered and worth remembering, people will in fact remember. Memory is a two-edged sword: the preacher remembers, which empowers the hearers to remember as well.

> In observing life, keep an eye out for that which is memorable.

The study of Life is, however, more than a search for memorable sermon material, and should never be reduced to that. I have often assigned fiction reading to preaching classes, telling them to read short stories, in order to cultivate a taste for the great communicators. One time a student told me that she had given up the stories and started reading Kahlil Gibran instead, because "I wasn't getting any sermon illustrations from the short stories." My answer was that reading fiction was assigned for its own sake, not for its value for deriving sermons. There is nothing more crass than the preacher skimming through books and magazines on Saturday afternoon in search of something to put in Sunday's sermon. That preacher might as well subscribe to one or more of the various sermon help publications — if you want canned sermon material, it doesn't make any difference who canned it. We do not read John Updike or Salman Rushdie or Barbara Kingsolver — not to mention Shakespeare, Tolstoy, or Conrad — to find sermon illustrations; we read because the books are worth reading in themselves; they have literary merit and tell us something about Life apart from any value they may have as fodder for Sunday. Yes, on occasion our living and observing may yield something that is easily remembered and to the point — then by all means, use it. But the study of Life is mostly background work, which goes not so much to the preacher's material needs but the preacher's character and credibility. Who would you rather listen to, someone who knows Life deeply, or someone who learns Life only in soundbites?

Life being what it is, and we being preachers, we will every now and then come across something in the living and observing of Life that cries out to be put in a sermon. When we do, we will then evaluate it: is it really appropriate for a sermon, and does it belong in this Sunday's sermon? Some material we will judge to be inappropriate, even though it might be otherwise worthy. Pastoral confidences are never appropriate for pulpit publication; they should forever be kept in confidence (you may be tempted to think you can get away with telling the story from past pastoral encounters at your next church, but apart from the possibility that word may somehow slink back to the old church that we have betrayed a trust, think of the effect on pastoral ministry in your present church, now that they know you are a blabbermouth). Personal stories, whether about yourself or your family, should also raise red flags; telling stories about yourself may send the wrong message — that the sermon is about the preacher and not about the gospel — and if you embarrass your family in public, they may have something to say later! Further judgments about the appropriateness of material can be made in light of the congregation and its situation — sometimes the seemingly perfect sermon illustration is too dark, too light-hearted, or otherwise something that people cannot readily hear at this place and time. There is no substitute for the preacher's taste and familiarity with the people in evaluating such material.

Assuming the material is appropriate, does it belong in this particular sermon? The answer may be no; sometimes the answer is found only after the sermon is written, revised, and rehearsed, and something seems dreadfully wrong — the sermon is over-long, perhaps, or seems overdone. If the sermon sounds and works better with the material cut, then cut. Save the illustration or example for later.

In order to save the material, the preacher must have some means of storage and retrieval. There are many different filing systems available to preachers; you can actually go out and buy one designed just for sermon composition. My own approach is simple, because I believe that the more complex the system, the less likely I'll be able to find it when I need it. My filing system consists of a computer file and a clippings file. The computer file is one word processing document (naturally called "File"), in which I occasionally write down short quotes and the like, along with the date. The advantage of keeping the file on a computer is that it is easily searched (the preacher cannot always rely purely on memory). In dealing with computer files, a word to the wise: backup. The clippings file is a standard hanging file in which I deposit articles from magazines and newspapers that are too long to be typed or scanned into the computer File. I lump them all together in one file, because it is easier to search through one file when I am looking for something, than to search in several places. Again, you will have to consider your own work habits as a preacher, and the media of your material; for example, those who surf the Web for a great deal of material may find it helpful to keep a disk directory devoted to downloaded pages (again: backup!). The important thing is to find a way to keep material at hand, using a system that works for you.

> Develop some means of storage and retrieval of material taken from your study of Life: a file, a box, whatever works for you.

Our study of Life has not prepared us for the Sunday sermon until we have narrowed it to the congregation at hand. Your congregation is to be considered only after a study of general humanity, lest you and your sermon become parochial. I used to tell preaching students to gear their sermons to the congregation at hand, i.e., the preaching class. What I got was a lot of, "We've left our homes and jobs to spend three years in this place" — sermons that were so narrowly focused that they were bad practice. It's too easy to preach to yourself and your friends, and no way to prepare for the real job facing one who must go into the pulpit week after week, year after year. To speak the word "we" without accuracy is to lose that part of the audience that does not see itself as part of the "we." I started telling my students to consider their congregation to be the class, the teacher, and one stranger who just came in off the street for a listen. Keeping the stranger in mind helped the students — as it will help any of us — keep the sermon from becoming too self-centered, self-indulgent, and yes, too parochial.

Yet it is essential to consider the actual congregation as the preacher knows it. There are specific exercises that will help the preacher study the congregation in preparation for Sunday. One simple exercise is to begin sermon composition with a list of concerns — the thoughts and issues that come to mind, be they personal, communal, or congregational. Simply list what is going on in your heart and mind. This will help clear the cobwebs, particularly of any personal issues that may get in the way of the sermon. It will also help you focus on what the situation is in your community, the world, and your congregation in particular. Once you are done with your list, set it aside; you can come back to it after composing your first draft of the sermon. Another way to study the congregation before composing the sermon is to do a thought exercise: picture the congregation before you on a Sunday morning — the people who usually sit to the left, center, right, front, back. Go through the pews in your mind, see the faces, name the names. Often this exercise will help the preacher be specific as well as sensitive: you will not be tempted to offer glib advice to Ethel who is undergoing radiation therapy, nor will you rant on about the problem with corporate capitalism and "business today" before Joe, who has been downsized and long ago ran out of unemployment benefits and most of his hope. If preachers need to study Life as a whole in order to keep themselves and their congregations from becoming ingrown, they also need to study the faces that commonly sit in the pew, in order to keep from being so general that they become vague, irrelevant, and insensitive.

Scripture

Once we have studied Life, examined our lives, and gotten in touch with the lives of our communities and congregations, we are ready to open our Bibles. In studying Scripture, however, we are not turning our backs on the study of Life. Far from it. We merely shift our gaze. Scripture never stands in and of itself, but always finds its life in the life of the Christian community. Even in the solitude of the study, the preacher reads with the community looking over the shoulder. The preacher's reading of Scripture is embedded not only in the preacher's personal inclinations and predilections, but in theological and denominational tradition, as well as the customs and history of a particular congregation.

Scripture is always read in community; there is no interpretation without presuppositions. Not only is pure objectivity in scriptural interpretation impossible, it is far from desirable. The preacher's job is to speak not only *to* but *for* a particular people. Preaching is a dialogue, in which Scripture speaks in interaction with a tradition, a congregation, and the preacher's own theological perceptions. None of these exist apart from the other — there would be no denominational or theological tradition apart from Scripture, no congregation apart from Scripture understood within that tradition, and no preacher, were there not a congregation to recognize and commission the preaching ministry. Scripture itself would not exist as Scripture apart from the believing community; without the Church, the Bible would be scrolls mentioned by religion textbooks in passing, nothing more — no more significant than the documents of ancient Egyptian or Aztec religion, and no more studied.

> Scripture is always read in community. Embrace your community and your tradition.

The communal embedding of scriptural interpretation is of crucial concern for those who would preach without a net. Since our sermon delivery must be funneled through our memory, our sermon study looks in particular for content that is memorable. Tradition is the firm post that memory leans on. Where would

Lutherans be without law/gospel duality, Presbyterians without the sovereignty of God, Methodists without John Wesley, Episcopalians without the Prayer Book, Baptists without the independent congregation, Roman Catholics without seven sacraments? These traditions can be evoked concisely, because they are so ingrained. The familiar is a memory aid. People rarely remember the outlandishly unfamiliar, because they have no reference point, no common denominator that lends a friendly hand to the mind. If I give a lecture and bombard you with new facts, new terminology, and new ways of looking at things, how much are you likely to remember the next day? However, if in my lecture I use terminology you already know, and show how a quite common idea can be expanded or changed in light of new evidence, I will gain a greater hearing, simply because I have moved from the familiar to the innovative. I cannot move in the other direction, nor can I expect you to take in more than a smidgen of totally unfamiliar material — I might as well be speaking in a language you do not understand. Our theological, denominational, and congregational histories can be of great help to us when we rely on them to provide familiar and memorable springboards to our preaching.

I am assuming that the preacher has received formal training in his or her theological tradition, as well as the broader contours of Christian tradition. Preaching has not been and never will be the exclusive domain of the seminary-educated, but the enthusiasm of youth is no substitute for the wisdom of the ages. Formal training allows the preacher the time and means to become grounded in the myriad disciplines that enhance one's preaching (including, under the best of circumstances, the study of biblical languages). There is no substitute for those years spent in library stacks and seminar rooms. Nor is there a better context in which to struggle with the great theological questions, the complexities of Christian history, and the multifaceted nature of the Scriptures. To deal honestly with the difficult issues of the faith requires time, and it requires a supportive place with sympathetic colleagues and teachers. Not that the preacher will ever tell the congregation everything learned in seminary — keep in mind the years spent mastering the theological disciplines, in contrast to the few minutes available for the sermon on Sunday. A full theological education cannot be delivered in sermons; that's why you went to seminary. Besides, as I have already noted, the technical language learned in seminary is unsuited to communication from the pulpit. You cannot mouth Greek or Hebrew words and expect people to hear more than "Abracadabra." The point of a theological education is to give the preacher tools with which to think. How else can this one person speak not only *to* but *for* the entire community? The preacher knows much more than is said on Sunday; he or she is in that sense over-prepared, the better to speak with authority. Over-preparation also helps us to speak wisely and deliberately, for we are able to pick and choose from a storehouse of knowledge, a large rather than piddling selection of facts. A liberal arts college education, followed by seminary training, best prepares one who would preach without a net.

Scriptural study for the preacher is of two types. The first is background — the broader study of Scripture as a whole that takes place as part of the preacher's wider continuing education. Learning does not stop with formal training, and most churches have wisely built in time and incentives for their pastors to participate in continuing education, whether from books, seminars, retreats, or distance learning. Part of that continuing education time will be spent with Scripture. The preacher may decide to learn more about a particular book

> Scripture study includes ongoing continuing education for background purposes as well as the study of this week's readings.

of the Bible — perhaps this year's gospel, if he or she is following the lectionary. Topical study — of a biblical theme, or of a line of history — can also prove helpful. Again, the purpose here is not to come up with sermon material per se (though it may result in a pulpit gem or two). This is merely a part of the preacher's over-training. We know more than we say, in order to speak wisely and with authority.

Continuing education can also save preachers from mistakes. Biblical studies is not a static field; there is always movement, and as with all the humanities, always influence from the broader culture. It is easy to spot a preacher who stopped studying at a certain point. Unfortunately for homiletics, there are certain misconceptions about the Bible that have a regrettably long shelf life (perhaps because they are particularly appealing). Not long ago I heard a sermon centered on the notion of God as "Abba," an ancient Aramaic term which was taken by the preacher to mean "Daddy" — the warm address of a helpless child to a kind and familiar face. This notion, launched decades ago by a famous biblical scholar, has been shown to have no linguistic basis, but the preacher was distressed when I sent him a copy of an article whose title said it all, " 'Abba' Isn't 'Daddy.' " "How was I supposed to know?" said the preacher. Continuing education, my friend. Another popular misconception is that there is a special biblical word that signifies the love of God (*agape,* or as a verb, *agapao*). Again, this is bad linguistics: words do not have inherent meanings — they mean things only when put into sentences. Plus, the basic thesis can be disproved quickly with a concordance. While *agape* and *agapao* are often used to refer to the love of God, they are not the only Greek words used for divine love in the Bible, and they are not used exclusively for that kind of love. In John 21, for example, Jesus uses *agapao* with its synonym *phileo* to explore Peter's love for him; there is no apparent difference in meaning between the two verbs. In Luke 11:43, the Pharisees are said to "love (*agapao*) to have the seat of honor in the synagogues and to be greeted with respect in the marketplaces" — hardly a divine love. Believe it or not, in the Greek Old Testament, *agape* and *agapao* are used in the context of rape (2 Samuel 13:1-19).

There is something to be said for basic legwork in Scripture study. A good many questions about the Bible can be answered with that most basic of tools, the analytical concordance. This is more than merely a list of all the English words in the Bible, since being "analytical" it also lists all the Greek and Hebrew words that underlie the English; thus it is a tool that will help the preacher understand the linguistic issues of biblical translation. A number of common misconceptions about biblical language can be cured with an analytical concordance. For example, are there really three root words in the Greek New Testament that mean "love," as we so often hear? No — the word *eros* is never used in the New Testament. Does *agape* ever refer to something other than the attitude of "love"? Yes — it refers to Christian table fellowship (2 Peter 2:13; Jude 12). Are there different Hebrew words that correspond to the various Greek words for love? Not really — the usual word for "love" in the Old Testament is *ahav*, though "love" is sometimes used to translate a few other words. All this information can be found quickly using a standard analytical concordance. It is accessible to the English-only reader through transliteration (the Greek and Hebrew words are spelled out in the English alphabet), though its use is enhanced by some familiarity with Greek and Hebrew.

This is why, despite the lowering of seminary standards over the years, as "practical" courses have crowded their way into the traditional theological curriculum, there is still an argument for an early and thorough education in Greek and Hebrew — it is not a matter of pinning a student's pastoral potential to linguistic ability, but of preparing the preacher as thoroughly as possible to be the best preacher possible. The study of biblical languages, preferably in college, is primarily helpful to the preacher in this sort of background work; few of us are linguistically gifted to the point that we will regularly pick up and read Greek or Hebrew during the preaching work week, but this sort of training opens up avenues of study that are simply not available to those who have not studied the languages. It also usually cures us of those simplistic notions about the language of the Bible — sometimes bordering on magic — that too many preachers and their hearers seem to share. In one of my all-time favorite sermons, the preacher declared that in a certain passage, "the word 'all' means *all*" — those of you who have been treated to more than one of those "this word really means ..." sermons will chuckle. Knowing biblical languages usually does not pin God down — quite the opposite, since it opens us up to possibilities of meaning we cannot see in translation.

Before we leave the topic of the preacher's ongoing education, it might be helpful to address the issue of books. The working preacher is apt to echo the writer of Ecclesiastes, "Of making many books there is no end, and much study is a weariness of the flesh" (Ecclesiastes 12:12); we may well be tempted to look at our stacks and shelves of unread books and cry, "Vanity of vanities, all is vanity!" As with many areas of the preaching life, there is a certain discipline that can help the preacher keep order. Resist the temptation to go hog wild at conference book displays; do not attempt to put every new commentary on one's shelf.

> Buy reference books carefully, beginning with the basics. Choose a good commentary over a prefab sermon resource booklet.

Look before you leap into the bookstore — particularly at reviews in periodicals; try to find out what are the best books on a subject, and what books educated people are talking about. Many periodicals now have their reviews online, so informed opinion is more easily accessible — but this is a two-edged sword, since there are many more online sites that are totally democratic and allow any crackpot (and there are many crackpots online when it comes to the Bible) to recommend (or pan) anything.

When it comes to choosing books for preaching preparation, the preacher should begin with the basics and move out from there. By "the basics," I mean a good study Bible with notes and cross-references, an analytical concordance, a one-volume Bible commentary, and a Bible dictionary or encyclopedia. Beyond these, the preacher will naturally begin to accumulate Bible commentaries. I do not recommend buying complete sets of commentaries, but individual volumes as needed. In particular, I would advise the preacher to find those one or two volumes that have set the agenda for the study of a particular book; these are the books that come along once every decade or two, which the others debate or imitate. A careful selection here, aided by competent reviewers, will put years of profitable study possibilities on the preacher's shelf, and lessen or eliminate the times when the preacher looks around the study and says, "Oh, why did I ever buy *that*?" When in doubt, try borrowing a particular commentary from a friend, or from a library; test it to see if it works for you. Careful attention to

50

a good commentary may enable the preacher to scratch some of those prefab sermon help booklets from the budget (much as I hate to say it, as an author in one such series!) — while these publications can be helpful at certain points in the sermon process (particularly later in the week as the preacher moves closer to the actual sermon), much of the biblical background material in them is redundant if one is using a good commentary.

The second type of Scripture study for the preacher is weekly sermon preparation. I am assuming that the preacher is going to deal with specific passages of Scripture in the sermon, even if a topical approach is taken. The topical sermon is not an excuse to cruise willy-nilly through the concordance, alighting gently on dozens of scriptural texts without ever boring deeply into one. The people of God are not nourished by glancing superficial blows from the sword of the Spirit — they are probably not even wounded by them, because nothing cuts deeply enough. Concordance preaching *seems* biblical enough — the preacher certainly quotes the Bible often enough — but lacks the depth of coverage that would make it *truly* biblical. This is by no means exclusively the fault of a topical approach — the preacher who deals with the Bible in course, and the preacher who uses the lectionary, may both be tempted to stay in the shallow end of Scripture. But they cannot expect their congregations to swim, if they merely wade.

The first task for the preacher in weekly scriptural study is to narrow the task to manageable proportions. The lectionary preacher has the task in part already decided, since lectionaries divide the Scriptures into bite-size chunks; there remains only to decide if the sermon will focus on Old Testament, Psalm, Epistle, or Gospel readings, or a combination — and whether the lectionary authors have sensibly chosen the starting and ending points of the passage (more on this later). Those who preach the Bible in course (whether verse-by-verse, paragraph-by-paragraph, or chapter-by-chapter) also have it fairly easy, simply taking the next section — though it might be sensible on occasion to evaluate the chosen divisions, to see whether they truly express the shape and contours of the biblical book, since verses, paragraphs, and chapters are all later accretions from various translators and editors, not part of the canonical text. The topical preacher may well have the hardest job at the point of selection of text, depending on the topic — there may be either an overabundance of texts to choose from (if the topic is, say, "love"), or an almost total dearth of direct references (if the topic is contemporary). In either case, the topical preacher needs to find and delimit those sections of Scripture that have the greatest bearing on the issue at hand.

It should be noted that there is no inherent reason for the Christian preacher to favor any one sort of method — lectionary, in-course, or topical — of selecting texts for preaching, since there are arguments pro and con for each, and each draws on a rich tradition. Much of the decision will depend on denominational and theological preferences. Liturgical churches use lectionaries, which are specifically designed to fit with the various seasons. What lectionaries cannot provide is the sense of continuity within the biblical books that preaching in-course gives; plus, there are certain large parts of the Bible that lectionaries skip entirely. However, in-course preachers can be equally guilty of favoring certain sections of the Bible. Topical preachers may sacrifice both liturgical relevance and biblical continuity, but if the topic is pressing enough, topical selection can focus the congregation more clearly than the other methods. There is a long history of effective preaching in all the different methods, and perhaps the best suggestion is for the preacher to adhere to the one best fitting the congregation, while keeping the others as options when the occasion demands. The illustrations that follow draw on the lectionary preaching tradition, since they come from my own preaching work; those of you from other traditions can make appropriate adjustments as needed.

Beginning preachers may wonder how much time they will be spending in Scripture study each week, and how that time is to be divided. I have already mentioned my general rule of thumb — approximately one-half of our sermon preparation time is to be spent in study. How that breaks down during the week is up to the preacher, but I would suggest that several smaller blocks throughout the week are better than cramming all our work into one day (especially if that day is at the end of the week!). Smaller blocks of study are beneficial for several reasons: they allow us to concentrate on a single task for a short while, and then take a break, thus reducing fatigue, and they allow our unconscious minds to take over in the intervals between study blocks. Preaching is often as much intuition as sweat, and so the process works best when it is given the maximum amount of space. I always start my preaching study on Monday, and spread it out over the week in chunks, usually of no more than an hour-and-a-half, in order to let my mind wander over the subject at the greatest possible length, but without overload.

> Spread your Scripture study out over the week, beginning with the weightiest references and moving progressively through easier material as you head toward the end of the week.

The key to developing successful study habits is to make it manageable. The beginner should be realistic about what can be accomplished in one week. Perhaps one cannot do in-depth study of all four lectionary readings for one week; instead, work through the notes in your study Bible for all the passages, but choose one to be the focus of your sermon and the object of more intense study. In three years, the lectionary will come around again, and you will have the chance to work through those other passages (and the study Bible notes will have given you a head start). Perhaps it will be too much to consult two or three major commentaries on a passage; again, in three years you will have another crack at these passages, so it might be best to focus on one commentary this year, and save the other for next time.

It is also appropriate to consider our study habits in light of how close we are to actually preaching the sermon; the tome that is manageable on Monday may seem far too heavy on Thursday. Generally, I reserve commentaries that are thick and technical for the early part of the week, thinner and more popular commentaries for the middle of the week, and sermon helps and preaching publications for the end of the week. As I move closer to sermon time, I want my resources to reflect more and more the modern world that the sermon will address.

As with the study of Life, the study of Scripture calls for the keeping of files. It makes no sense for the preacher to spend hours with head in book, but have nothing to show for it later but a sermon manuscript. The working-smarter preacher will keep notes on what is studied during the week, knowing that the lectionary will come around to this same passage again in three years, that the next section of the Bible preached in-course may well refer back to this passage, or that the topics covered in this passage will come up in the future. There is simply no good reason not to keep and file study notes. In fact, I believe that the preacher should make note file creation the primary act of study. The weekly study of Scripture becomes largely a matter of keeping one's files.

> The weekly study of Scripture is largely a matter of keeping files, so that we can use them again for another sermon later.

I am going to suggest that the preacher keep very specific sorts of files. These should be computer files for all but the most Luddite among us; we are going to be using and reusing these files over the years, and the computer offers the most flexibility for adding to and changing these files (need I say again: backup). The confirmed Luddite need not feel excluded, however, since the same system may be followed using a loose-leaf notebook, and a separate sheet of paper for each major section. The preacher will keep files of two sorts: text files, and index/reference files.

Index/reference files deal with individual biblical books. They are "reference" files of material dealing with the individual books in a general way. This is the place to keep notes from your study Bible or Bible dictionary — outlines, background material, historical context, information about the original author and community. Reference files enable the preacher to get back on board with a particular biblical book in a quick and concise manner — you might not immediately remember what the Book of Joel is about, but a glance at the Joel reference file will remind you that Joel is a

Philippians Index
Phil 1:1-11: Adven2no.yrc
Phil 1:21-27: Prop20no.yra
Phil 2:1-13: Prop21no.ra
Phil 3:7-14: EpiphLno.yra
Phil 3:8-14: Lent05no.yrc
Phil 3:14-21: Prop22no.yra
Phil 3:17—4:1: Lent01no.yrc
Phil 4:4-7 (8-9): Adven3no.yrc
Phil 4:4-13: Prop23no.yra

Philippians Reference
[Ronald Hock in HSB (HarperCollins Study Bible)]
Author and Recipients
    Paul visited Philippi c. 50 C.E. (Acts 16:11-40) during
        second missionary journey, founded church (cf. 1:8;
        2:19, 24)
Place and Date
    Paul in prison (1:7, 13-14, 17) but no note of where (cf. 2
        Cor 11:23)
    Traditionally assumed to be Rome (1:13; 4:22), but not
        necessarily — could be Caesarea (Acts 23:23—26:32),
        Corinth, or Epheus
    Probably written late 50s or early 60s
Integrity of Letter
etc.

Figure 1

response to a devastating locust plague. This is not the same as simply looking up "Joel" once more in your Bible dictionary — the reference file format allows the preacher to gather together and synthesize background material from many sources — for example, is there a debate on where Paul's letter to the Philippians was written? Your reference file will know. The reference file is also used as an "index" file, because you use it to index your text files; all the text files that refer to this particular book of the Bible

Phil 1:1-11

Paul and Timothy, servants of Christ Jesus, to all the saints in Christ Jesus who are in Philippi, with the bishops and deacons. Grace to you and peace from God our Father and the Lord Jesus Christ. I thank my God every time I remember you, constantly praying with joy in every one of my prayers for all of you, because of your sharing in the gospel from the first day until now. I am confident of this, that the one who began a good work among you will bring it to completion by the day of Jesus Christ. It is right for me to think this way about all of you, because you hold me in your heart, for all of you share in God's grace with me, both in my imprisonment and in the defense and confirmation of the gospel. For God is my witness, how I long for all of you with the compassion of Christ Jesus. And this is my prayer, that your love may overflow more and more with knowledge and full insight to help you to determine what is best, so that in the day of Christ you may be pure and blameless, having produced the harvest of righteousness that comes through Jesus Christ for the glory and praise of God.

Context:

Source:

Form:

Text:

Content:
v. 1   Paul and Timothy, servants of Christ Jesus, to all the saints in Christ Jesus who are in Philippi, with the bishops and deacons.
v. 2   etc.

Comment:

Says:
Does:

Figure 2

56

are listed here — again, so that the preacher never has to duplicate study that has already been done (Fig. 1).

Text files deal with specific texts from the biblical books. My text files are arranged according to the lectionary (thus they have names like Lent01NoYrA, for "Lent 1 Notes, Year A"). Each file has the same format, which follows the method I use to study the text (Fig. 2). In other words, the file format helps me move through all the steps necessary to successfully engage the text for preaching: the passage itself, its context, form, source, text, verse-by-verse content, comments, and summing-up statements (I'll deal with each of these in what follows). The file repeats this format for each reading: Old Testament, Psalm, Epistle, Gospel, plus leaves room for general notes and concerns. I set up a basic template for all my preaching notes; once I have the template set up for a particular Sunday, I can reuse the same file every time that lectionary selection reoccurs. Since I have the index files, I can also copy and paste individual passages that occur more than once in the lectionary to other text files as needed. I set aside some time once every few months to prepare templates for a couple of months ahead of time — if I have preached on that Sunday before, it is merely a matter of changing the date and making sure the file format is up-to-date; for a new template, I will copy the scriptural texts into the template and format them for use (electronic lectionary texts and Bibles are widely available — you don't have to type it in yourself). I've found that actually having the complete lectionary text (in bold print) in the text file is a great aid to the sermon study process; I am easily reminded of the entire biblical text I will be preaching. I copy the text twice — once in a block at the head of the notes, for easy reading, and again with verse numbers in the "Content" section, for verse-by-verse notes. I use an informal outline style (with no letters or numbers) rather than paragraphs for notes; each section uses hanging indentation, with subsections further indented — I find this style makes it easy to find a particular piece of information and anything related to it (see the sample sermon text file included at the end of this chapter).

Over the years, I've learned to make notes that are complete rather than sketchy, i.e., full sentences rather than suggestive phrases, because I don't want to puzzle over cryptic communication three years later when I reopen the file. As with all my note files, I try to make it as useful and transparent as possible for repeated use. There are no footnotes or bulky scholarly apparatus, but I do keep track of sources, both so I know what I have already looked at, and so that I might refer to it again if necessary. I usually cite the source by author's name and page number for commentaries, or by simple abbreviations for common reference works (if there is any doubt about the abbreviation, I cite the title in full the first time I use it). It simply has to be clear enough that I know later where it came from. Sometimes I will even include complete quotations from commentaries and secondary sources, if they are particularly well-phrased and memorable. The point is, make the notes usable and helpful for you, thinking not only of this week but of future use. Recognize that you don't have to put everything in there right now; your notes will accumulate over the course of years, as you come back to these passages again and again.

Once this Sunday's text file has been set up, the preacher is ready to begin the weekly study process — we are now ready to work on our files. I suggest that the next step be a direct encounter with the chosen biblical text. This is as much a meditative exercise as an academic one — of course we will want to familiarize ourselves with the basic content of the text, but we also want to approach it in a spirit of prayer and openness to God, keeping our ultimate purpose in mind. We are here to discover a word from God; we must find it for ourselves before we can present it to our people. Later will come a time to bury ourselves in the minutiae of exegetical studies, but at some time we must reemerge from the ancient world to speak to people who have dragged themselves out of the work week and into the pew — our final task will be that much easier if we begin with the end, knowing before we start that we seek something not just for our minds but for our souls.

The first reading is quiet, prayerful, and explorative. It begins with the translation we will read in church on Sunday morning, then perhaps moves to the original languages (if such is our facility) or other translations. Our notes at this point go in the "Comment" section of our file (or perhaps "Content," if they are connected to a particular verse). Any musings and/or exploratory ideas for the sermon go into our notes. Perhaps nothing we note at this first step in the process will make it into the sermon — but who knows, something memorable may occur to us by God's grace, and we had best set it down before we forget it! More likely, these early notes will contain questions: What don't we know that we need to know to understand this passage? What doesn't make sense at first glance? What needs more puzzling? Chances are, if the preacher has such questions on first reading, the congregation will have similar questions — thus our initial questions may provide the basis for a sermon. Only time will tell, but since we will need our memory for more crucial work, we had best jot down those initial questions (if we're working on a computer and it seems silly later, we can always press delete!). There are many possibilities that may occur during the first reading, and many ways of doing it. The beginner will want to be very deliberate about the first reading, noting all the possibilities; with repeated practice, a natural and instinctive approach will soon develop.

Once our first reading is complete, and our notes in the file, it is time to save the file and take a break before we launch into the main section of our file work. The break is not just a chance to relax mind and body, but allows our subconscious to take over the sermon process — who knows what will pop out when next we open our files? (Whatever pops out, it goes into the file; it may not make it into this Sunday's sermon, but there are other Sundays, and we will be using this file again.)

Our template will guide us into the work needed to complete our file this week: we will want to observe the passage's context, source, form, text, and content; then we will make comments and sum up what we have learned about the passage. I will explain each task in order.

Context. While there are various theological conceptions of the inspiration of Scripture, no thinking Christian believes that the Bible was dropped into our laps directly from heaven. Every biblical passage has a context. It is more accurate to say that it has *contexts* — a literary context, as it exists not in isolation but as part of a larger written work; a theological context, as that larger writing has a particular theological perspective, else it would not have been read and preserved by the Church; a historical context, because the writing arose from a specific person who lived in a specific place and time and wrote for a specific audience; and an anthropological and a sociological context, because that writer was a human being and immersed inextricably in and among a particular group of other human beings. These contexts are distinguishable for analysis yet in actual practice are bound together — we are, after all, dealing with a piece of literature, from which we must deduce the historical, theological, anthropological, and sociological contexts. Really, all we have are words. We've got to figure out the rest. Fortunately, smart people have been thinking about these issues for a long time, so we don't have to go it alone.

> For each Scripture reading, pay attention to context, source, form, and text, as well as the actual content.

It is best, however, to start with the words themselves. To determine the literary context, read what comes before and what comes after the passage selected for Sunday. How does this day's reading fit into the whole? Does it advance the story or argument? Does it introduce something new? If we are using a lectionary selection, does the selection contain an entire and complete unit, or has it cut off something crucial at the beginning or end (or even cut something important out of the middle)? My general observation is that lectionaries can do very poor jobs of choosing where to start and end a particular reading, often chopping off a hand or a foot or even the head of a particular passage (especially when the material in question has been deemed too confusing for sensitive modern congregations). I frequently find myself appending verses (in small but bold print) to the beginning and ending of my "Content" section, as well as making notes under "Context," so that I might have the broadest possible view of the literary context as I look over my notes (I also routinely include in my text files verses that have been omitted by the lectionary in the middle of a passage, again in small bold type). In many cases, however, the literary context involves a section too large to be read aloud on a Sunday, and so the preacher will begin to consider ways to help the congregation place the reading within its larger literary context — who can preach on a passage from Jonah without telling the whole story? Who can make sense of the conversion of Cornelius without recounting the entire movement in the Book of Acts from a Jewish to a Gentile Church? Romans 9-11 cannot be truly understood unless it is seen as the climax of the argument made in chapters 1-8. Even at this early point in the sermon process, it may become clear that certain material will have to appear in the sermon, if the congregation is going to understand how the biblical story or argument holds together as a whole.

The preacher can learn much from the words of Scripture, and even more from those who have read them with care, so it is now time to open the reference books. We need the books to tell us not only if we have done a good job of discerning the literary context of our passage, but to tell us things that require a broader knowledge of the text and its time and place — the theological, historical, anthropological, and sociological context. Again, there is no magic here — knowledge about these matters does not drop out of the sky, but is the result of attentive reading of biblical and other texts, along with relevant material from other disciplines, such as archaeology. We rely on the writings of scholars not to supplant but to supplement our own reading of the biblical texts — our reference books enhance what we have gleaned from our own observations. This is to say that every reference book is read *critically*, because every scholar writes in his or her own literary, theological, historical, anthropological, and sociological context, and every argument must be evaluated against the evidence of the text, and against other likely suppositions. Since the basis of any argument about Scripture is the text itself — to which we preachers have the same access as any scholar, particularly if we read the original languages — we each have not only the ability but the necessity to evaluate our references. A particular scholar may have incorrect information, incomplete information, draw faulty conclusions, or make tenuous applications of the facts. On many issues, there is more than one plausible way of looking at things.

This is why we do not rely on only one scholar or group of scholars for our reference files, but seek opinions from a broad point of view. This we accomplish over time — we cannot cover everything about this one passage this one week, so we will begin with basic information that can be expanded and enhanced as time goes by. Our weekly study is simply one extension of our lifelong continuing education.

A good place to begin working on the theological, historical, anthropological, and sociological contexts is your own reference file on the particular book of the Bible being read this week — and if you don't have one, it is time to create one! The reference file contains general information that can be gleaned from study Bibles, dictionaries, and encyclopedias, and the introductions to commentaries. Things like authorship, date, place, possible audiences, and book outlines — material that deals with the various contexts of the book in general — go into the reference file. Then material that is relevant to the passage in question can be copied and pasted into your text file. (Don't forget to enter this week's passage and filename into the index before you close your reference file!) Attention to details at this stage pays dividends later. Even the seemingly obvious should be noted, lest one be caught flat-footed when a parishioner asks a question like, "Where exactly *was* Philippi?" — notes from our study Bible or dictionary will tell us not only the location, but what the city and its Christian community were like.

While we are not looking for specific sermon content at this stage of the study process (remember, this is part of our *over*education, so that we can speak authoritatively without a net), there may be a sermon gem that comes from studying the contexts. Often there is one particular piece of contextual information that the congregation will need in order to understand exactly what is going on in a particular part of the Bible. Joel's locust plague is but one example — Joel's vision of the Day of the Lord is couched in imagery derived from the biology of hungry grasshoppers, whose swarms block out the sun and cover houses and fields, consuming every bite of food that is not sealed airtight. Who can understand

Paul's words against idols in 1 Corinthians 8-10 without understanding the ancient meat-markets, which sold food that had been offered to idols in the pagan temples? Often this was the only meat one could find, and since meat itself was an expensive luxury, Christians in Corinth were faced with the possibility that a host's extravagant hospitality may pose a spiritual danger — if not to oneself, then maybe to a weaker brother or sister. Recent studies into the social dynamics of the Corinthian church suggest that a good deal of the problem at Corinth had to do with the varied social composition of the community; perhaps the battles at Corinth were not so much about theology but about class and money, and thus their disputes over food, clothes, and status spilled over into liturgy, ethics, and doctrine. These are only a few examples of how understanding the contexts can open up an entire text. Sometimes that one literary, theological, historical, anthropological, or sociological gem may be the pivot on which the sermon will turn.

It will become obvious to anyone who has worked in this way for a few weeks that our division of the various tasks of interpretation will not always correspond to the ordering of the material we find in our reference works — here we are working on the historical context, when the book goes off and says something about source or form, or makes a crystal observation that needs to be attached to a particular verse! Needless to say, at such times we move to the appropriate section in our file and make the note there. The advantage of using the computer or loose-leaf folder is that we can leave a bookmark, add or change something elsewhere, and come back to where we were. We can make the material work in our way, for us rather than against us.

Source. Just as the Bible did not drop overnight into our laps, neither did the words simply drop from heaven into the pens of its authors. The diversity of Scripture lies not only in its many books that stem from different places and times, but also in the many sources that went into the making of those books. Behind a great number of biblical books lies a complex history of composition, which may include oral transmission of material, written sources, and various stages of editing. Some of the biblical sources are explicitly cited: "Now the rest of the acts of Rehoboam, and all that he did, are they not written in the Book of the Annals of the Kings of Judah?" (1 Kings 14:29; cf. 11:41; 14:19; 15:7, 23, 31; 16:5, 14; 22:45). Others have been plausibly reconstructed by scholars. It is clear, for example, that Matthew, Mark, and Luke share one or more common written sources, since their wording and order is often identical. The dominant thesis is that Matthew and Luke used Mark and a common sayings source, but a vocal minority of scholars argue for a different configuration — and none of the various hypotheses is without problems.

Source analysis is where we sometimes find the greatest differences among scholars, and where the theological leanings of those scholars are most influential. This is because sources are not patently obvious, and easily become a template for what one would like to believe. Theological conservatives sometimes argue against source theories or pseudonymous authorship of biblical writings, because their theories of biblical inspiration and authority require them to. Similarly, theological liberals sometimes divide biblical books into various sources in order to prove that the canonical writings distorted the essence of the original faith, which must be replaced with something else. In both cases, it may be difficult to tell the chicken from the egg — did the theology inspire the source theory, or vice versa? Both extremes may be recorded in our notes, but we will look for more moderate voices to evaluate them. In particular, we will look for literary rather than theological arguments to justify source theories — a source theory must enable us to make more sense out of the final form of an ancient document, not less. We will also look for consensus views on these issues, on the theory that great agreement indicates the more compelling theses, while widespread disagreement means that we are looking at something that could go either way.

In recent years many source theories have come under fire from sophisticated literary analyses. Features of texts that older scholars had taken as source seams can now be seen as indicators of the literary shape of the book. For example, it has long been held that chapter 21 of the Gospel of John is a later appendix to the original book that concluded with 20:30-31. Scholars argued that the narrator's voice in 20:30-31 gave a distinct note of finality, that the "many other signs" mentioned referred to the whole of Jesus' ministry, and that chapter 21 is anticlimactic, contains non-Johannine language, and is entirely too ecclesiastic in focus. But a minority of scholars have argued that there are good literary reasons to see chapter 21 as a piece with the rest. On this view, 20:30-31 is a conclusion to that chapter, not the Gospel as a whole; it is one of many such intrusions of authorial commentary (cf. 2:22; 11:51-52; 12:16; 19:34-35). The "signs" referred to are the signs of chapter 20, those Jesus performed after his resurrection in order to compel faith. The difference in language in chapter 21 is explained by the subject matter (it's the only fishing scene in the Gospel), and the chapter is no more ecclesiastical in focus than the rest of the Gospel (cf. 14:12; 15:12-27; 17:17-18, 20; 19:26-27). As for chapter 21 being anticlimactic, that is in the eye of the beholder; we could argue that the chapter provides a necessary conclusion to themes introduced earlier in the Gospel concerning the future of the community founded by Jesus. The real question here is whether a source theory or an argument for literary unity best explains the text before us — what helps us make most sense of the Gospel of John as a whole? Note that even if we decide that John 21 is of a piece with the rest of the Gospel, we are not able from this to make any claims about who wrote it — we are not endorsing the ancient tradition that John the son of Zebedee was the author, which must be decided on other grounds. Similarly, scholars may argue over Wellhausen's division of the Pentateuch into J, E, P, and D sources, but outside of certain theological conservatives, none of them is claiming that there were no sources, or that Moses wrote it all.

Commentaries may or may not emphasize source theories, depending on their depth, theological leanings, and audience. The fatter, more technical commentaries generally have more discussion of sources than more popular volumes. Some books, such as the Pentateuch, some of the Prophets, and the Gospels, lend themselves to discussion of sources, because there is a wealth of comparative material, while with other books any discussion of sources is entirely hypothetical (did Paul quote early Christian hymns in his letters? If only we had an early Christian hymnbook!). Sometimes the issue of sources is bound up with the broader issue of authorship; if, as most scholars believe, many of the Pauline letters were written by later disciples, how much of Paul's own writing did they incorporate? Again, we are not looking for certainty here, which we will not find; we are looking for consensus among scholars, and for the most convincing arguments.

As always, preachers will do well to approach the issue of sources for themselves. This is not as daunting as it may seem — there is no magic here, but simply the same skills applied in other areas of biblical interpretation: the careful reading, comparison, and evaluation of texts. The preacher could, for example, open a synopsis of the Gospels, which sets the various books in parallel columns, in order to compare this Sunday's Luke with Matthew and Mark. Where are they the same, where are they different? How might we account for the similarities and differences? This is not merely an academic exercise, but can yield homiletical fruit. For example, in the resurrection narratives in Mark and Matthew, the message to the women at the tomb is "Go, tell": "Go, tell his disciples and Peter that he is going ahead of you to Galilee; there you will see him, just as he told you" (Mark 16:7); "Go quickly and tell his disciples, 'He has been risen from the dead, and indeed he is going ahead of you to Galilee; there you will see him.' This is my message for you" (Matthew 28:7). But in Luke, there is no "Go, tell"; instead, the women are told, "Remember": "Remember how he told you, while he was still in Galilee, that the Son of Man must be handed over to sinners, and be crucified, and on the third day rise again" (Luke 24:6-7). The entire thrust of the message is different in Luke. The resurrection is not new information that requires speedy communication. It is simply a matter of remembering what Jesus has already taught them. This verse links to Luke's theme of the fulfillment of Scripture in Jesus and the early church. For Luke, God's plan was foretold long ago and needs only to be disseminated by faithful teaching. The preacher who is not inspired along these lines may find another tack in the command to "Remember": it was given to *women,* not the male disciples, which indicates that they were present during Jesus'

66

teaching sessions. In other words, Luke pictures the women as disciples in their own right, not just as messengers for the males. Why is knowing the sources important to the sermon? As I have already noted, sometimes source theory gives a clue to the sermon. But even if source theory does not directly contribute to Sunday morning, it is necessary background work, because it helps us understand the distinctiveness of each biblical book, how it was put together, and how it hangs together. Most of all, source theory helps keep preachers honest. It would have been easier if the Bible were obviously dropped from heaven, unambiguously a divine and not a human production. But this is not the Bible we are dealing with, nor has our God chosen to work this way. God speaks through frail and imperfect human beings, using every facet of our humanity. The Word is made flesh. So we read the Bible for what it is, not for what we want it to be.

Form. Sometimes it's not *what* we say that counts, but *how* we say it. We've all had experiences in which how something is said actually determines the content of what is said. If you say, "I'll love you forever," and I respond by saying, "I love you, too," while whipping out a prenuptial agreement and a pen, I've said it all. The confession transcript may read, "Yeah, I did it," but it makes all the difference to the jury whether I said those words weeping hysterically or with a sarcastic grin on my face. The distinction we are making is between form and content, between what we say and the way we say it. We are able to make the distinction for purposes of analysis, but in actual practice, the two are indistinguishable. You cannot have form without content. You cannot have content without form. Form specifies content.

Form is a matter of function. It has to do with the *how* of communication, what a speech or a piece of writing *does* as opposed to what it actually says. Ideally, there is a harmony of form and content, because we choose forms that fit the content — what we say fits in with what we intend to accomplish with those words. If I want to send you a letter, I choose the appropriate form, and begin, "Dear John." If I want you to sign a contract, I write, "The party of the first part...." If I want to amuse you, I begin with, "Did you hear the one about...." I miscommunicate if I choose a form that is inappropriate for the content; I don't tell the joke during the opera, or at a funeral. If I want to proclaim my undying love, I do not send a contract, but if I intend to do business with you, yet mail you a love letter, I may not only lose your business but run afoul of the law.

Unfortunately for those who study the Bible, written communication lacks many of the formal clues that make face-to-face and verbal communication clear. We can't look Paul in the face to see if he's being serious or playful. We can't hear the inflection of his voice, in order to understand whether he is asking a question or making a statement (this is no small matter, since Paul's Greek included no punctuation marks). Written communication is of a completely different order for this reason: we are limited to the writing itself for any formal clues that may help us determine its meaning.

Nevertheless, readers are not left at sea when it comes to form and function. There are certain formal features in writing that help us understand function. I've already mentioned some of them. "Dear John" indicates a letter. "The party of the first part" indicates a contract. Writing is a social convention; we have to follow certain ways of putting words on paper in order for other people to understand fully what we have written.

The biblical books themselves take on particular forms of all sorts. Even a cursory glance at the Bible shows the variety of forms found there: history, poetry, prophecy, narrative, apocalypse, letters, and possibly even fiction (I've always wondered about Job and Jonah). Each of these different forms communicates in different ways. Genesis tells us a story; the Psalms generally do not. Psalms evoke our emotions; the Proverbs, our minds. Where the Gospels communicate their theology by means of narrative, the letters of Paul give us theology embedded in the lives of particular Christian churches. Each form does something different to us; each communicates according to its own function.

Within individual biblical books there are various forms of smaller scope. For example, scholars have long noticed that Gospels are made up primarily of short stories strung together like pearls on a string, interspersed with blocks of teaching material.

The various stories are of different formal types, according to their purpose, and we can categorize those types. The "pronouncement story" is based on an ancient form called the *chreia*; it is a brief story, similar in form to a joke, in which there is a setting, action, and a concluding saying of significance (the "pronouncement"). Miracle, healing, and exorcism stories in the Gospels seem to follow set patterns every time they appear. The sayings of Jesus are also variously categorized according to form and function as logia or wisdom sayings, prophetic and apocalyptic sayings, community rules, "I"-sayings, and parables.

As we shall see, form is a matter of both structure and language, arrangement and style. We begin a letter with particular words, "Dear John." But we expect the letter to follow a certain arrangement: address, greeting, body, salutation. Ancient letters followed similar conventions both in terms of structure and language. Thus Paul's letters always begin with a variation on the standard Greco-Roman epistolary opening, "Paul to Philemon, greetings." But Paul has transformed the standard form in order to effect his theological purpose, so the greeting is expanded to, "Paul, a prisoner of Christ Jesus, and Timothy our brother, to Philemon our dear friend and co-worker, to Apphia our sister, to Archippus our fellow soldier, and to the church in your house: Grace to you and peace from God our Father and the Lord Jesus Christ" (Philemon 1-3). Not only is the wording of Paul's greeting predictable, but the structure of the entire letter will follow a standard format. The greeting is typically followed by a "thanksgiving period" which recounts the main themes of the letter (cf. Philemon 4-7). Then follows the body of the letter, which sets forth the main lines of what Paul has to say (Philemon 8-16). Paul will conclude with an exhortation (Philemon 17-22), convey further greetings (Philemon 23), and a final blessing (Philemon 25). Once we determine the structural features of each Pauline letter, we will have a better idea of how our particular passage for this Sunday fits in with the whole.

Attention to ancient formal conventions can spare us from a number of mistakes in biblical interpretation. In New Testament studies, there is a tendency to fall back on "mirror interpretations," that is, to assume that whatever is said in the text holds a mirror up to the author's original situation — whatever is said, someone else must have been saying the opposite. If I say "A," then my opponents must have been saying "Not-A." This is particularly true in Pauline studies, where we are hampered by having only one part of a multi-voice conversation. To some extent, the "mirror interpretation" reflects a sound method: if Paul tells us that his opponents have said such-and-such, we should take him seriously. At other times, however, this method can disguise a laziness in the examination of form. For example, Paul begins chapter 6 of Romans with, "What then are we to say? Should we continue in sin in order that grace may abound?" It might be tempting to believe that Paul was speaking against certain people who claimed that sin was a conduit to grace. However, if we read Romans for its larger formal features, we will find unmistakable traces of an ancient rhetorical form called the *diatribe*. One of the formal features of the ancient diatribe was the use of questions posed by an imaginary opponent that provide a springboard for the next point of the author's argument. A quick glance over the text of Romans will find many such questions (cf. 3:1, 5, 9, 27; 4:1, 9, 10; 6:1, 15; 7:7, 13). They are not a feature of Paul's human opposition, but of his chosen rhetorical form.

Why is form important? As we have already noted, it can make all the difference in how the content is perceived. Knowledge of the larger form helps put a particular passage in the proper literary context. And form can clue us in to the writing's larger purpose. There is no way to separate form and content, so we ignore formal features to our peril.

Biblical forms can also help the preacher form the sermon itself. We are going to face the same task of communication as the original biblical author: here is some content about the nature of God that has to be conveyed to the community. Why cannot we preachers learn from how the biblical authors themselves set forth the message? Their form could be our form. This is not to say that a sermon on a Psalm would take the exact form of a Psalm, or that Paul's diatribe would become our diatribe. We must choose forms that are appropriate to our time and place. The thing to consider with each form is, what does it do? What is the function of this form? In the case of the Psalm, we might conclude that the function is to express our deepest thoughts and emotions to God. The sermon on the Psalm that takes the Psalm's form seriously would be a worshipful expression of thoughts and emotions. If we were to preach on Paul, we would ask about the function of the diatribe form. Well, obviously Paul chose the form because he wished to make a logical argument. The sermon that takes Paul's form seriously would appeal to the mind and make the connections between ideas clear. What we would *not* do is try to make an argument out of a Psalm, or get mushy with Paul. Paul's content did not lend itself to the Psalm form. What the Psalmist had to say about God and humanity could not be expressed as an argument. We ignore the form to our peril, both as biblical interpreters and as preachers.

Text. We now turn to the process of determining the original text, or textual criticism. Many biblical scholars place this step closer to the beginning of the process, as it is logically prior to some of the issues we have already discussed. And in fact, I often move directly to this step after my first meditative reading, because I find that it gets the juices flowing. I place it here, however, because it is a highly technical issue that is not readily accessible to those who read the Bible in translation. Of primary importance to scholars and translators, it is a lesser yet sometimes necessary step for Sunday's preacher.

Textual criticism is commonly misunderstood by beginners. It has nothing to do with translation. It is the process by which scholars determine what the original biblical authors wrote — the actual Greek or Hebrew words that were first penned on a scroll. In the age of the printing press, it may be hard to remember that books were once copied by hand. In the age of acid-free paper and temperature-controlled libraries, it may be hard to believe that scrolls wore out quickly. None of the biblical writings survive in their original forms; we do not have the scrolls that contain the handwriting of Paul or Luke. The only way to publish a book in the ancient world was to make copies by hand. These copies did not last long, unless they were kept dry (this is why those famous manuscript discoveries always happen in the desert); we do not have any copies of the New Testament that go back to the first century, and the earliest copies of the Hebrew Bible date centuries after composition. Many of our earliest copies of the biblical books are merely fragments.

When you copy by hand, mistakes inevitably creep in. Fortunately, we have a great many handwritten copies of the New Testament books (fewer for the Hebrew Bible). We can compare these manuscripts, and take into account the various ages of the materials, according to handwriting styles and scientific tests. Scholars have come up with a variety of rules for judging how close a particular manuscript comes to the original, and how many mistakes have crept in over the years. The rules work quite well. For example, we have all had the experience of typing something from a book or from handwriting, and accidentally skipping a line or two because of an identical word or phrase. Handcopyists were prone to the same kinds of error. (We don't have time or space to cover all the rules of textual criticism here, but there are a number of good introductions to the subject.)

By careful examination and comparison of the available manuscripts, scholars have determined the most probably original text of the Bible; the resulting "critical text" is the foundation of all reputable modern translations. While there are a great number of textual variants among the various manuscripts, the good news is that the great majority of them are a matter of Greek syntax and linguistic variants that have little bearing on meaning or translation. All the variants are important to scholars and translators, but only a relatively few make a difference between translating a sentence this way or that. It is with that minority of significant variants that the preacher must be concerned.

Beginners who read in translation often have trouble differentiating textual variants from translation variants. Textual variants have to do with differences in wording in the original language; translation variants have to do with different possibilities for translating the same Greek or Hebrew word. In this step, we are concerned only with textual variants — only with the process of determining as best we can the original Greek or Hebrew text. This is because the criteria for evaluating textual variants are different from evaluating translation variants. With a textual variant, the only question is which word the author more likely put down (and he could have written only one word), and we will have to decide the question based on the rules of textual criticism. But a translation variant gives us an instance of one word that could mean one thing, another, or possibly both things at once — and our decision will be a purely interpretive one. Thus textual variants are noted differently from translation variants in modern Bibles. Typically, the footnote for a textual variant will say something like, "Some ancient authorities read...." A translation variant is indicated simply by "Or...." In other words, if the footnote does not mention an ancient authority or manuscript, it is talking about a translation variant, which will concern us when we deal with the verse-by-verse content, but not here. Translation variants have nothing to do with textual criticism.

Obviously, textual criticism is difficult for those who have no facility in the original languages; even the reference books on the subject may be difficult. The thicker and more technical commentaries often deal extensively with textual variants, but they assume a certain familiarity with the process. Again, most textual variants involve minor matters, and so are not noted in the average translation; the preacher can be satisfied that only those textual variants that are worth a footnote in the translation are worth the preacher's attention. These significant variants will receive attention in the commentaries, so the preacher who works only in translation will not lack for a reliable authority. Often there will be no textual variants in this week's scriptural passage that are significant enough to merit a translator's footnote, so the preacher will be able to complete this section quickly by writing "No major variants cited in translation."

Why then should a preacher bother with this highly technical process of textual criticism, especially when most of the variants are relatively insignificant? The answer is that sometimes it makes all the difference in the world. The most obvious example is the ending of the Gospel of Mark. Most Bible translations include a "Shorter Ending of Mark" and a "Longer Ending of Mark" at the end of chapter 16; the longer ending actually has verse numbers

(vv. 9-20) and may not even be set apart from the previous section in some translations. The overwhelming consensus of biblical scholars, however, is that Mark ended at chapter 16, verse 8, and that both of these endings are later additions, added by another editor. This is not speculation, but a result of careful textual criticism. The oldest and most accurate biblical manuscripts of Mark end with 16:8. Many manuscripts include 16:9-20, the "Longer Ending." Some also include the "Shorter Ending," placed in various positions. Some have only the "Shorter Ending." The differing positions of the various endings indicates that they are a result of later fiddling with the text — some of the ancient manuscripts even have marginal notes that say the endings are doubtful! Thus when the preacher rises to preach Easter morning on Mark 16:1-8, textual criticism will make a great deal of difference to that sermon — the preacher is dealing with the end of Mark's story, not a chapter to be continued.

It must also be said that while preachers tend to use modern translations, in many churches there are Bible readers in the pews who prefer the King James Version. What they do not realize is that the King James Version is based on pre-critical Greek and Hebrew texts, and so contains many errors. In the King James, Mark 16:9-20 is included as part of the text, no footnotes. The preacher who deals with Mark 16:1-8 as the end of Mark's story on Easter morning needs to acknowledge that the traditional text contains this extra material, and explain why. Otherwise, the preacher may lose credibility — "I can see for myself that it doesn't end there. What's wrong with that preacher?"

In the end, the preacher must pay attention to textual criticism, however technical and difficult it may be at times, because this is the nature of the biblical text given to us. It is necessary for us to know about it when the question comes up, but most of all, it is necessary for us to be honest about the kind of Bible with which we have to do.

Content. The "Content" section is where I keep notes on a verse-by-verse basis. Here is where I put items that do not fit the above categories, as well as things that are particularly tied to one section of the text. The bulk of what the preacher gleans from the commentaries goes here — commentaries, after all, are usually arranged verse-by-verse. I tend to think of this section of the text file as a place that gradually gathers data, and thus expands as knowledge increases. If the template is blank, I begin with the notes from my study Bible, and items from Bible dictionaries. Next I will take up one commentary and work through my notes using it. If I have time this week, I may take up a second commentary for comparison and contrast. If not, I can always return to the file with a new commentary three years hence, when the lectionary cycle returns to this passage.

Comments. This is a section for general comments that do not fit any of the above categories. It may contain the questions and musings that came with the first meditative reading, as well as thoughts that may have accumulated during or at the end of the process. Here is also where I will take down memorable quotes from commentaries and secondary sources, particularly those that have to do with how to preach the passage. Once we have gotten to the "Comments" portion of the text file, we have moved close to the turning point in our study; it is almost time to return to the modern world.

Lectionary preachers may want to add an additional "Comments" section to the very end of their text files, after all the readings for the day have been dealt with in turn, in order to record thoughts about how the different readings interact. Here is also the place to record memorable quotations from lectionary resources that deal with all the lections. This section can be very valuable for those sermons that deal with more than one passage of Scripture. Again, what you write here may or may not make it into Sunday's sermon, but you will have the chance to come back to it in years to come.

Says/Does Sentences. Before we leave the biblical world to return to our own, we need to sum up what we have learned. This is a necessary final step that we may often be tempted to skip. We have learned so much in our week of study, how could we possibly reduce it to a sentence? Yet it is precisely because we have learned so much that we need to give it focus. Without this final step, our scriptural study remains a conglomeration of facts, figures, and suppositions grouped around a certain scriptural passage. By writing down a summation, we integrate all this material under a single heading — or in this case, two headings.

We write two summary sentences at this point in our study. These are short, simple, positive declarative statements. The first summary sentence concerns content — what the text says (thus I call it the "Says" statement). The second sentence concerns form — what the text does (the "Does" statement). We need both, because as we have already seen, form and content are inseparable, and both help us with the sermon. Content has its obvious bearing on the pulpit — we are going to defend, expand, debate, clarify, and/or argue with what the biblical text has to say. But the biblical form — what the text does — will also help us frame the sermon; we will make an argument, bestow a blessing, or tell a parable, depending on what form and function the biblical text itself has used to weave its web of meaning.

> Summarize your study of each passage with two sentences, dealing with content and form. Answer these questions: What does the text say? What does the text do?

Another way of looking at the Says/Does statements is simply to ask, when all is said and done and the Scripture is read and reread, the fundamental question: What does God have to say here, and how does God say it? We are looking for the central thrust of the passage, not a tangent, not some peripheral item that somewhere along the way looked like it might preach. Most of all, we are looking for something that speaks to us as preachers, and as human beings under God. Chances are, if it does not speak in some way to us, it will not speak to our people. Our study has not been merely an academic exercise, but our own search for that Word which touches us deeply enough to form the basis of the sermon. If it does not preach to us, how could we possibly preach it to others? Ultimately, what we are summing up in the Says/Does statements is our own encounter with God through the text. As with the study of Life, there may be moments in our study of Scripture when study turns into prayer. There is no need to quench the Spirit at such a time; this is the reason we came into this place.

Once we have composed our Says and Does statements, it is time again to take a break, and let our subconscious feed the sermon process.

From Study To Composition

The next major step after study is composition. We have learned all we can learn for this week; we have explored *what* we will say. The next step is to consider *how* to say it. Our content will take on a certain form, which is the sermon itself. Composition will be the subject of the next chapter; here we will consider how we manage the transition between study and composition.

The movement between study and composition may not be obvious. Our study has immersed us deeply in an ancient world. The concerns of Corinthians may not be transparent to modern people (who buys meat at pagan temples these days?), and the preacher dare not make the mistake of assuming that the congregation has been in the same careful attendance to the Scripture as the preacher has this week — I dare say that when they walk into the church on Sunday, most of the congregation is only barely aware that there is such a thing as Scripture — their week has been absorbed elsewhere. The preacher is going to have to lead them gently by the hand into the world of Scripture. Thus we began our study with the study of Life, because we are going to have to start in the congregation's world, in order to bring them into God's world.

In some sense, the move from study to composition is simply a change in audience. In Scripture study, the audience was ourselves and those like us — the preacher, a trained observer of Life and Scripture, in conversation with like-minded scholars. In composition, the audience is non-specialized — simply people who have walked in off the street, who don't necessarily know anything about the Bible, or Greek or Hebrew or source theory or

> The move from study to composition is simply a change in audience. Prepare to compose the sermon by imagining your congregation as the new audience of your study.

textual criticism. The preacher speaks the vocabulary of the specialist, while the people, if they know that language at all, do not use it on a regular basis. The preacher goes into study hungry for a sermon; the people go into church hungry for a word from God. The movement from study to composition is a change from a community of scholars, an audience of biblical specialists, to a general audience of those who have come hoping to hear something that might change their lives.

So the preacher cannot move directly from Says/Does statements to the pulpit. There needs to be some rearranging of the mental furniture. We have struggled hard to get inside the mind of Paul; now we must get back inside the mind of Ethel and Joe and the others — some of whom we may never know, not even their names — who will be sitting in the pew, waiting for our words. By now it will become apparent why we began our study with Life and not with Scripture; the study of Life overshadowed our entire voyage back into the world of Scripture, and now will enable our return to the present. Now is the time to think back over the reflections and concerns with which we began this whole process.

The movement between study and composition is enhanced by various brainstorming processes. These are throwaway exercises that help get the juices flowing. I usually do these in a comfortable chair, away from my computer and bookshelves, with pen and paper — I may come up with something that should go into my text file later, but for now I simply want my mind to roam over the territory. One brainstorming exercise involves the Says/Does statements: these are statements about the ancient world of the biblical text — how might I rephrase these in modern terms? The same could be done with the successive sentences of the biblical text itself — the Bible says this, what are some modern analogies? Another brainstorming exercise is to circle a word or phrase in the biblical text, and consider the modern images it evokes. I usually keep a list before me of areas I might consider in relation to the word or phrase: music, theology, literature, film, history, current events, personal experience, or congregational experience. I am simply looking for analogies, illustrations, examples, or even structures that will help me move from the specialized audience of biblical studies to the audience I will actually face from the pulpit. Anything that occurs to me, I will write down — this is brainstorming, not yet composition — and I may or may not find that material useable in the end.

As I consider the movement towards composition, I will remember my ultimate purpose. I am here to proclaim a word from God. Scripture is the basis of that word, but God speaks in many ways and in many places. My hearers are not theologians but ordinary people who hunger for the divine. Like any good rhetorician, I wish to touch the heart, head, and will of my audience; I will present them with the facts, but I want their emotions and desires as well. Nevertheless, I am not required to be clever or witty on Sunday; clever and witty will serve my purpose if I have the opportunity to call on them, but my job is to be a faithful proclaimer of God's good news. In the end, all I have at my disposal for this task are the words conveyed by my body, one person to a roomful of others. Like a trapeze artist, I will be working without a net — which is to say, I have nothing to fall back on but God. Preaching is an act of worship, in that it relies on our total dependence on God.

Thus even at this stage, I need to consider not only the congregation's profit and delight, but my own. The congruence of the sermon with the preacher's emotions is essential for a spontaneous delivery, and it begins at the beginning. I simply cannot preach what I do not believe; I cannot proclaim as good news that which makes me yawn. Here is another thing that separates the preacher from the actor: the actor utters another's words, while the preacher speaks his or her own, but the actor is acting — the preacher must be the real thing. One of the keys to preaching without a net is to re-experience the sermon as it is preached. The sermon in some sense reenacts the word delivered to the preacher.

> **Begin sermon composition with the theme sentence, a short, simple, declarative statement of what the sermon will be about.**

This requires a genuine encounter with God. You cannot re-experience that which you never felt at all. We have already seen that there may be moments during our study of Life and of Scripture when study dissolves into prayer. The preacher may also experience such moments during the brainstorming process, as study moves toward composition. As before, these moments fuel not only our preaching, but also our souls.

The movement between study and composition will conclude with the first act of composition, the theme sentence. This is a short, simple, declarative statement of what the sermon will be about. Once we have written this statement, we know the content — we know *what* the sermon is going to be about. Before we proceed to form — *how* we are going to say it — it is time for another break in order to rest the body and let our subconscious mind go to work. If we are lucky, and God is gracious, our minds will present us with a sermon form when next we sit down to continue our work. The sermon is always a gift from God, but there are those special weeks when we give thanks because the gift comes both brightly wrapped and easily opened.

Appendix to Chapter 2:
Sample Text File

Luke 21:25-31 (Advent 1, Year C)

Jesus said, "There will be signs in the sun, the moon, and the stars, and on the earth distress among nations confused by the roaring of the sea and the waves. People will faint from fear and foreboding of what is coming upon the world, for the powers of the heavens will be shaken. Then they will see 'the Son of Man coming in a cloud' with power and great glory. Now when these things begin to take place, stand up and raise your heads, because your redemption is drawing near." Then he told them a parable: "Look at the fig tree and all the trees; as soon as they sprout leaves you can see for yourselves and know that summer is already near. So also, when you see these things taking place, you know that the kingdom of God is near."

Context:

    Luke's Gospel is first volume of two-volume work including Acts. Traditionally thought to be authored by Dr. Luke (Colossians 4:14; 2 Timothy 4:11; Philemon 24), but this is impossible to prove or disprove. Generally the book is dated to the last third of the first century; there are definite allusions to the destruction of Jerusalem (70 C.E.). While there is some debate, Luke-Acts seems to be written for a largely Gentile church.

    Literary context: this passage is part of Lukan apocalypse in chap. 21

        Luke gives audience as "some," sets speech in Temple (21:5-7, 37-38)

        Jerusalem to be surrounded by armies, v. 20

        People flee, vv. 21-23

        Dead and Captives, Jerusalem trampled by Gentiles until time of Gentiles fulfilled, v. 24

        vv. 25-31 today's lection

        v. 32 This generation will not pass away

v. 33 Heaven and earth will pass away, but not my words
v. 34-36 Exhortation to be alert
NRSV paragraphs vv. 25-28, 29-33, 34-36
Headings in HSB (*HarperCollins Study Bible*):
    Destruction of Temple Foretold 21:5-19
    Destruction of Jerusalem Foretold 21:20-24
    Coming of the Son of Man 21:25-38
Fitzmyer [*Luke,* 1334] sees discourse in two parts:
    a) vv. 8-24: What will precede the end of Jerusalem
      (i) vv. 8-11, The Signs before the End
      (ii) vv. 12-19, Admonitions for the Coming Persecution
      (iii) vv. 20-24, The Desolation of Jerusalem
    b) vv. 25-36: What will precede the end of the world
      (i) vv. 25-28, The Coming of the Son of Man
      (ii) vv. 29-33, The Parable of the Fig Tree
      (iii) vv. 34-36, Concluding Exhortation to Vigilance
Johnson [*Luke,* 324] sees threefold temporal division:
    Times of Persecution (21:12-19)
    Times of Destruction of City (21:5-11, 20-24)
    Times of Son of Man (21:25-38)
Broader literary context takes us to second volume of Luke-Acts
    Luke's signs are fulfilled in Acts: a time of witnessing (vv. 12-19; cf. Acts 4-5; 24-26) [Craddock in HBC (*Harper's Bible Commentary*) 1039; cf. Johnson 326]
Luke's account of destruction of Temple reflects a historical event, rather than the more eschatological setting of Mark. Luke then puts the eschaton after "the times of the Gentiles" (v. 24), which may refer to Gentile mission. [Craddock in HBC 1039]. But NB that Luke still sees the parousia within his generation (v. 33) [though Johnson, 328, notes the figurative dimension of the evil "generation" in Luke 7:31; 9:41; 11:29, 30, 31, 32, 50, 51; 16:8; 17:25]
Questions: does Luke really write with the expectation of imminent parousia (a controversy that goes back to Conzelmann)? What does the answer tell us about Luke the

person, the community he lived in, and the historical situation underlying the Gospel?

Source:

Markan, with editing, and some relation to Q material in 17:20-37, and some L material

Sometimes the original version of this material has been considered to be from a Jewish or Christian apocalypse

Luke's account of destruction of Temple reflects clearly a historical event, in contrast to the more eschatological setting that Mark gives this discourse

Most significant Lukan changes (in 21:5-19): [Culpepper in NIB 9:398 (*New Interpreter's Bible*)]

1. Omitted reference to disciples as audience
2. Structure of three imperatives, vv. 8-9
3. Change from "but the end is still to come" (Mark 13:7) to "but the end will not follow immediately" (21:9)
4. List of signs in v. 11 expanded to include apocalyptic signs of parousia (21:25-36)
5. Reference to prisons foreshadows Acts
6. Luke omits "good news must first be proclaimed to all nations" (Mark 13:10)
7. Luke omits reference to Holy Spirit (Mark 13:11); Jesus will give them words
8. Luke adds assurance that not a hair will be lost from their heads (21:18; cf. 12:7)

Parallels are Matthew 24:29-33; Mark 13:24-29

v. 25 Luke reads "signs in sun and moon and stars" for sun and moon darkened, stars falling
Luke adds "on the earth distress...waves"

v. 26 Luke adds "men fainting with fear and with foreboding of what is coming on the world"

v. 27 Luke and Matt have single "cloud" for Mark's "clouds"; "power and great glory" rather than Mark's "great power and glory"
Luke omits gathering of elect by angels

v. 28 Lukan addition: "Now when these things begin to take place, look up..." Luke omits description of angels gathering the elect in Mark 13:27

v. 29 Only Luke cites fig tree as "a parable" Adds "and all the trees"

v. 30 Lukan variation in saying, "as they come out in leaf, you see for yourselves and know...."

v. 31 Luke alone reads "kingdom of God is near" for Mark/Matt "he is near, at the very gates"

Fitzmyer [1323-30] sees discourse as composite of isolated sayings; Luke based his work on Markan redaction, edited greatly, and added some L material

Form:

Apocalyptic sayings about Second Coming and its cosmic consequences

Parable embedded and cited as such

Text:

No major variants in NRSV or Metzger's *Textual Commentary on the Greek New Testament*

Content:

v. 25 **"There will be signs in the sun, the moon, and the stars, and on the earth distress among nations confused by the roaring of the sea and the waves.**

Signs in the sun, moon, stars: Luke changes Matt/Mark wording. Luke omits Mark's "in those days," thus separating the destruction of Jerusalem from the parousia. Luke "lacks any temporal reference or time-table.... The time of final judgment is left completely undetermined and unattached to any tumultuous events in Palestine." [Johnson 330; cf. Fitzmyer, contra Culpepper]

signs, *semeion,* in heaven were common in apocalyptic, cf. Joel 2:30-32; Isaiah 13:10; 34:4; Ezekiel 32:7 [HSB]. Cf. Luke 21:10-11. Jesus' enemies (11:16) and disciples (v. 7) had asked for a "sign"

on the earth distress among nations: vv. 25b-26b are Lukan addition. Possible allusion to Isaiah 24:19; cf. Psalm 65:8

Terrestrial problems added to cosmic signs. "By shifting attention to cosmic signs and the panic 'among nations,' Luke introduces a larger end-time drama than that involving Jerusalem" [Johnson 327]

confused by roaring, waves: "The entire cosmos will be disturbed, radically affecting human life everywhere" [Craddock in HBC 1039]. Possible allusion to Ps 46:4; cf. 89:10

v. 26 **People will faint from fear and foreboding of what is coming upon the world, for the powers of the heavens will be shaken.**

People will faint with fear... More of Lukan addition; cf. Isaiah 24:17-20; Josephus *Antiquities* 19.1.5

faint, *apopsucho*, "stop breathing," "collapse," or even "die" [Fitzmyer 1349; Johnson 327]. Cf. 4 Maccabees 15:18

things coming on the earth, *oikoumene*, cf. Acts 11:28. Further distinguishes destruction of world from destruction of Jerusalem [Fitzmyer 1350; cf. Johnson 328]

powers of heaven shaken: Here Luke agrees again with Matt/Mark. Possible allusion to Isaiah 34:4; Haggai 2:6, 21; cf. Acts 17:26

v. 27 **Then they will see 'the Son of Man coming in a cloud' with power and great glory.**

Then they will see the 'Son of Man coming in a cloud': cf. Daniel 7:13-14; Acts 1:11; Luke 9:26; 11:30; 12:8, 40; 17:22, 24, 26, 30; 18:8

with power and great glory: Luke follows Matt rather than Mark here

v. 28 **Now when these things begin to take place, stand up and raise your heads, because your redemption is drawing near."**

Now when you see these things: cf. v. 27; Acts 1:11. Luke omits Mark's description of angels gathering the elect (Mark 13:27)

stand up and raise your heads: "Jesus' followers are not to share the fear and foreboding mentioned in v. 26; in contrast, their attitude will be one of rising and upright, joyful expectation. They will stand to welcome their deliverance." [Fitzmyer 1350]

> "Those who endure, who bear witness, who remain alert in prayer, have nothing to fear from the coming of the Son of Man. For them there is not distress or confusion or dread. For them it is the time of 'liberation.' And they can therefore stand up straight, hold their heads high in happy anticipation before the Son of Man." [Johnson 330-31]

> **stand up,** *anakypto*, echoes description of crippled woman bound by Satan (13:11) [Johnson 328]

because your redemption is drawing near: cf. 1:68; 2:38; 24:21

> **redemption,** *apolutrosis,* "Redemption here is in the sense of rescue and not in its usual meaning of salvation by repentance and forgiveness." [Craddock in HBC 1039]. Cf. Rom 8:18-25. "Release," not "ransom" [Fitzmyer 1350]. NB that deliverance associated with parousia, not death and resurrection.

v. 29 **Then he told them a parable: "Look at the fig tree and all the trees;**

> **Then he told them a parable:** Luke calls it a "parable," while Matt/Mark have Jesus refer to a "lesson"
> Luke's short parables: 4:23; 5:36; 6:39

> **Look at the fig tree:** Draw a lesson from leaves and blossoms
> Cf. parable of barren fig tree (13:6-9)
> Fig tree often used as metaphor for peace and prosperity of Israel (Deuteronomy 8:7-8; Hosea 9:10; Micah 4:4)

> **and all the trees:** Lukan addition, in recognition that example is not limited to figs — "a rhetorical extension" [Fitzmyer 1352]
> Or may be reference to Gentiles (fig tree = "Israel") [Culpepper in NIB 9:408]

v. 30 **as soon as they sprout leaves you can see for yourselves and know that summer is already near.**

as soon as the leaves sprout: or "when they put forth," no object in Gk

you can see for yourselves: Lukan addition, stresses that no further extension needed [Fitzmyer 1353]. "The visible emergence of the leaves makes it possible for anyone to draw the proper conclusion about the coming of summer" [Johnson 328]

and know that summer is already near: Returns to Markan form; young leaves are the sign of summer and its fruit; cf. "summer fruit" in Amos 8:1-2

v. 31 **So also, when you see these things taking place, you know that the kingdom of God is near."**

so also... Draws the conclusion of the parable — "As surely as one can discern the approach of summer by the leafing of a fig tree, so these signs announce the nearness of the kingdom" [Craddock in HBC 1039]

the kingdom of God is near: Matt/Mark read "he is near, at the very gates"

kingdom of God: cf. 21:31; 10:9, 11

Luke allegorizes the parable: the kingdom is as near as summer, and comes as surely as the leaves [Fitzmyer 1353]. Cf. 10:8, 11; 19:11

Lukan tension: Kingdom is present in words, works of Jesus, but not fully realized (10:9, 11; 22:16-18) [Johnson 328]

Comments:

Luke wrote for an age when apocalyptic thought reigned — but is our age any different?

Note for further study: what do we mean by "apocalyptic" in the Lukan context, and how is that the same or different from our own?

Says: The coming of the Son of Man brings redemption.

Does: Foretells, promises, terrifies, teaches, shows signs.

Compose

In a nutshell: Sermon composition includes choosing both memorable structures and memorable language. We are composing for oral presentation, and our writing will reflect the oral nature of our final product. I suggest using an "oral manuscript form" to facilitate rehearsal and revision.

One who preaches without a net must have something memorable to say. The preacher must also say it in a memorable way. The two are separate yet inseparable. Memorable content can and will die without memorable form. Memorable form that has nothing memorable to say will kill any interest in a congregation — perhaps impeding them from hearing that preacher for years to come, since boring is more easily forgivable than shallow. Neither will do for one who wishes to preach without a net, simply because we want to preach good news in a spontaneous style, and spontaneous rarely sounds boring, while good news is never shallow. To proclaim news that is really good is interesting in and of itself, but to say it memorably is to plant seeds that will grow thirty, sixty, and hundredfold.

As content and form are separate but equal, so form can be considered from two separate and equal angles: structure and language (thus Cicero's distinction between *arrangement* and *style*). One aspect of form deals with the ordering of material — how the parts fit in with the whole. Another formal aspect is the choice of words and how they are put together in sentences. The difference is, perhaps, one of scale: language is the microcosm of form; structure, the macrocosm. At any rate, both involve the single act of composition. Considering structure and language together as the dual aspects of form reins in the temptation to think of style as merely the embellishment of plain speaking, like decorations on a cake, or to think of structure as inconsequential for those who can turn a phrase with skill. Both aspects of form are essential to a memorable sermon composition.

Notice that I speak of "composition" and not "writing." You compose a sermon; you do not write it. You may (and under this system for preaching without a net, you definitely will) write a first draft of the sermon — i.e., put certain words down on a piece of paper (or a computer screen). But those words — papered or screened — will not be the sermon. The sermon is only, nothing more or less than, the words that are delivered to the congregation. Make no mistake about it, the sermon is never finished until it is preached; before Sunday morning, the question is not whether the sermon is done, but if it is ready to go. After Sunday morning, there is no sermon but the one that lives in the memory of the preacher and congregation. There may well be a written draft — smudged with corrections, revisions, and traces of the sweaty hands of the one who used these pieces of paper in rehearsal — but the draft is not the sermon itself, but merely the written remains waiting to be placed in its file-cabinet tomb. The sermon isn't there anymore; it's only a husk.

> You compose a sermon; you do not write it. The sermon is nothing more or less than the words that are delivered to the congregation.

We have already noted that the composition of the sermon formally begins with the theme sentence. This is a short, simple, declarative sentence of what the sermon is about. It is not an exhortation. It is not a refrain. It contains no metaphors, no twists nor turns of fancy rhetoric. It is simply an unembellished and bald statement of what the preacher is about this week. It is the answer to the question: What is your sermon going to say? Perhaps it is more accurate to say that the theme sentence is what your hearers will say when asked, "Give it to me straight and simple, short and not necessarily sweet, what did the preacher have to tell us?" The composition of the sermon begins with the theme sentence, short and simple. I should perhaps qualify this, since the theme sentence need not actually appear in the sermon itself. The purpose of the theme sentence is to give the preacher focus during composition. It has governing force. It is the *what* of the sermon, distilled — in that sense, it could be considered the last act of study as much as the first act of composition. Depending on the choices the preacher makes about form — the *how* of the sermon — the theme sentence in its original form may or may not make the final cut. Its purpose is not to survive the editing process intact, but to guide the preacher in terms of content. It does not in and of itself determine form. Thus it could be — and probably should be — quite prosaic in its own form. A metaphor in the theme statement might obscure the preacher's thinking enough to make the whole sermon fuzzy. Save the metaphor for the sermon itself. Keep the theme sentence pure.

A well-composed theme sentence that is allowed to govern the composition process gives the sermon the quality of *unity*: the sermon says one and only one thing. This is what the sermon is about. Every sermon needs to have one point — no more than one, no less than one. If something does not fit that one point, ruthlessly scratch it out of the sermon. Record it in your file for future use, but do not dare to put it in this week, less your sermon crumble into pieces. It cannot be emphasized too strongly — we write the theme sentence not as something to put in the sermon itself, even though we may do so, but in order to guide us into composing a sermon that says one thing. The purpose of the theme sentence is to clarify and guide the content of the sermon, giving it unity, a laser focus on one thing. Write your theme sentence on a card and tape it on the wall. Write it on a Post-It note and stick it to your computer monitor. Again, these are words that may or may not themselves actually appear in the body of the sermon — but they are intended to evoke the sermon.

If we are going to write the theme sentence into the sermon, it needs to go at the end, not the beginning. Write the theme sentence at the bottom of the page, not the top. This is because we want the sermon to have the quality of *anticipation*. If we blurt out the theme sentence at the beginning of the sermon, we have given our listeners no reason to listen to the rest of it. We have given them profit but no delight. It is food delivered in a hermetically sealed sack to a dinner party with noses clothespinned shut and mouths deadened by novocaine — nourishing, perhaps, but no fun. The sermon should be more like a gourmet meal, prepared in the next room by someone you love, the smells wafting in from the kitchen and stimulating the senses, while the assembled guests talk and laugh and look forward to eating soon. The theme sentence is a plain and blunt utensil because the preacher needs it to be; we don't use it to assault our congregation, but to prepare their feast. So it does not belong at the beginning of the sermon, but if anywhere, at the end. It is the *goal* of our preaching — where we want our congregation to end up, not to begin. The old preaching saw, "First I tell 'em what I'm going to tell 'em, then I tell 'em, then I tell 'em what I told 'em," is wrong precisely for this reason. It is a faulty approach to form, because it fails to build any anticipation into the sermon. It hits us over the head with the theme sentence, until we cry, "Uncle!"

The theme sentence is both the last act of study, since it will tell us what the sermon will be about, and the first act of composition, since it will help us develop a structure that has both unity and anticipation. A good theme sentence summarizes the *what* of the sermon while helping us with the *how*. But it will not determine our sermon structure for us. The next decision the preacher must make is how to arrange the material gleaned from a week of study.

Structure

For some preachers, the next step is to start writing the first line of the sermon, and continue on until the end. While this has the virtue of spontaneity, it is not the route we will take if we really want to *sound* spontaneous on Sunday morning, unless the preacher has a highly-developed intuitive sense of form. We run the danger of composing in uncertain and haphazard manner, confusing structural elements because we haven't thought the sermon through as a whole. Or we risk subjecting our congregations to a kind of deadening repetition — we don't think about structure, so we end up using the same structure by default week after week. The congregation quickly catches on: "Begins with a joke, ends with a teary story," and this relieves them from the obligation of listening. Form can be heard as content — if you always say it the same way, people may conclude that you are saying the same thing over and over again. Preachers need to consider sermon structure, if for no other reason than to keep their congregations on their toes.

Sermon structure makes all the difference in developing those two qualities we began to consider with the theme sentence: *unity* and *anticipation.* Structure can in and of itself create or destroy unity. The old "three points and a poem" sermon form was death to unity; built into the structure was the notion that we were going to say three different things, not one — there was nothing about the structure that demanded that the three points, or even the poem, be connected. How much better to choose a structure such as "Not This/But This." Clearly this sermon will have one main point; the preacher has half of it from the beginning, since obviously the theme sentence will serve to summarize "But This." If we must have a three-part movement, how about "Thesis/Antithesis/Synthesis"? At least the three parts will be linked. Unity is essential to the sermon — particularly for those who would preach without a net. One thing is more memorable than many, for both preacher and hearer.

We have already seen that considering the theme sentence as the goal of our sermon will help create anticipation. Anticipation is mostly a matter of structure, however. The sermon must have

> Sermon structures help create anticipation and unity; they are also memory aids.

that quality of the meal being prepared within smelling distance. We know where we are going — we're going to get to eat. But we don't get there all at once; we take some time to savor the preparation. The sermon must have a goal, or it will have no anticipation. But we must give them some hints along the way, or it is not anticipation but merely surprise. A proper choice of structure can help create anticipation, because it can build it into the very fabric of a sermon. If I choose as my structure, "Not This/Nor This/Nor This/But At Last This," I will have a hard time *not* creating anticipation! The same could be said for sermon structures that have a built-in twist, such as Lowry's "homiletical plot," or the "inductive" form that is designed specifically to lead to a certain conclusion. If you really wish to profit with delight, try to create anticipation, which means, pay attention to structure.

For the one who would preach without a net, there is another reason to look at structure before we leap. Our ability to preach in spontaneous fashion is going to depend on saying something memorable — and that begins with saying something we ourselves can remember. Often when preachers look at their draft manuscripts and say to themselves, "I could never remember all this," the fault is in the structure. The sermon form has unsightly bulges, tears in the fabric, signs of clumsy repair. A tight and well-considered sermon form is a memory aid. It not only makes the sermon more memorable for the hearers, but also for the preacher. "Today my sermon follows the Not This/But This form," we think as we step into the pulpit — how could we forget? Next week we will say, "This sermon takes six logical steps from beginning to end." Attention to structural form is attention to memory, and thus essential to preaching without a net.

> The preacher has three choices for structure: taking forms from the text of Scripture, using a prefab form, or inventing one's own.

When considering structure, the preacher has three choices: we can take our forms from the text of Scripture itself, we can use a prefab form, or we can invent our own. I'll consider each one in order.

Sometimes the ideal structure for a particular sermon is sitting right before us, in the text of Scripture itself. Augustine long ago suggested that we can learn to speak eloquently by observing the form of Scripture, and that applies to arrangement as well as style. Verse-by-verse preaching, as practiced by Augustine and many since, is but one example of using the form of Scripture to structure the sermon. Modern preachers who find the verse-by-verse procedure too much like a micro-manager may instead choose a paragraph-by-paragraph or section-by-section approach to the same advantage. Preachers who choose to retell a scriptural story in modern guise and have the story stand alone as the sermon are using the biblical form to structure their own in a very direct way. There can be more subtle ways of making use of the biblical structure; for example, an outline of the biblical form found in a commentary may suggest the steps the sermon might take. When we studied the biblical text, we took a special look at the structural form, and we summed up the formal attributes when we asked what the text *does*. It may well be that our sermon can *do* in the same way — the *how* of the text may tell us the *how* of the sermon.

The preacher may also choose a prefab structure. These are forms that have been widely used over the years for many kinds of speeches and other communication. Depending on the content of Sunday's sermon, one of the following might prove to be the perfect vehicle:

Identify/Evaluate/Offer
Explore/Explain/Apply
Exposition/Application/Exhortation
Appeal to Mind/To Emotion/To Will
Argument: Major Premise/Minor Premise/Conclusion
Outline: A/B/C/Conclusion
Inductive Outline (from the specific to the general)
Thesis/Antithesis/Synthesis
Problem/Solution
What It Is Not/What It Is
Not This/But This (Or Not This/Nor This/Nor This... But This)

Rebuttal: Common View/Truth
Either/Or
Both/And
What It Meant/What It Means
Lesser/Greater
Promise/Fulfillment
Ambiguity/Clarity
Facets: This Is True/And This/And This ...
Monologue: Questions/Answers
Dialogue
Chiasm (a/b/c/b'/a')
Story
Story/Reflection
Letter
Roman rhetorical form: Introduction/Statement of Case/Division of Headings/Constructive Arguments/Refutation of Opponents/Conclusion and Final Appeal.

There are also prefab structures that are sermon-specific. Some of these have been in use for years, others have been proposed recently by homileticians. Here are some of them; in the case of modern forms, I've noted the particular homileticians who have proposed them (see their books, listed in the appendix, for more specific information):

Traditional verse-by-verse form (ancient Greek homily)
Medieval "University Sermon" (similar to Roman rhetoric): Introduction/Prayer/Theme/Citation of Scripture Chapter and Verse/Division of Verse/Declaration (justifies the division)/ Grouping (illustrates the division)/Application
Law/Gospel (traditional Lutheran)
Puritan "Plain Style": Statement of Direction/Exposition/ Theological Analysis/Application
Traditional Topical Sermon: Description/Evaluation/Application
Quadrilateral Sermon: Scripture/Tradition/Experience/ Reason
Inductive Sermon: Awareness/Discovery/Exploration/Resolution (early Fred Craddock)

Biblical Text/Modern Story in mutual interpretation (Charles Rice)

Homiletical Plot or Narrative Form: Upsetting the Equilibrium/Analyzing the Discrepancy/Anticipating the Consequences/Disclosing the Key to Resolution/Experiencing the Gospel (Eugene Lowry, who concisely summarizes the form as Oops/Ugh/Aha/Whee/Yeah!)

Plot made up of Moves: Creating an image in congregational consciousness through a series of highly structured episodes (David Buttrick)

Four Pages: Trouble in the Bible/Trouble in the Word/Grace in the Bible/Grace in the World (Paul Scott Wilson)

Black Preaching: Text, Exposition and/or Narrative culminating in Celebration (African-American preaching, as exemplified by Henry Mitchell)

Sermon as Collection of Images (Thomas Troeger)

First Naiveté, Criticial Reflection, Second Naiveté (Ronald Allen, following philosopher Paul Ricoeur)

There is, however, something to be said for do-it-yourself sermon structure. Nothing prevents the preacher from creating his or her own structure for the sermon, and the advantage for one who would preach without a net is obvious: the structure is that much more memorable, because we created it ourselves! Many preachers do-it-themselves instinctively week after week, composing the sermon structure by intuition. For those who have never tried it, a simple procedure would be this: First of all, decide where you want to go. In other words, what is the conclusion of the sermon? (Hint: you've already written a theme sentence.) Second, once you've found your goal, pick a starting place. Where is the sensible place to begin if you are going to such-and-such a place? Ideally, the preacher will pick a starting point that easily relates to the congregation, on the theory that it is better to move from the familiar to the unfamiliar. Sum up your starting place in a sentence, much as you did with your theme sentence. Finally, decide what steps the sermon needs to take to get from here to there. Given that you're starting here, and ending up there, what are the spots in-between that you must pass through? Pick a manageable number of intermediary stops, and write a sentence summing up each one. Now, look at your sentences, see if they hold together as a whole, rearrange if necessary, and voila! you have a sermon structure. Now you can flesh out the various steps into a full-fledged sermon.

No matter how one chooses the structure for Sunday's sermon, the preacher should use a variety of structures. Listeners may say, "Wow!" when they hear a particularly innovative or unusual sermon form, but if they hear it again next week, they may well say, "Oh, no, not again!" Besides, no one form will work for every sermon idea, so it makes sense to look at different possibilities, and choose the one that best fits what we have to say this week. We need to look no further than Scripture itself to justify a diverse approach to sermon form — the biblical authors chose structures that were suited to what they had to say. As I have already noted, if we always use the same form, we may be *heard* as saying the same thing every time. This is a particular pitfall for those who routinely create their own structures — we may unconsciously be recreating the same form, over and over again.

Language

In our search for the most memorable sermon — we want to be able to remember it ourselves, in order to preach without a net, and such memory is aided when we say things that others will readily recall — the most important tool at our disposal is our use of language, what Cicero called *style*. If you think about memorable lines in the English language — ranging from Yogi Berra, "It ain't over 'til it's over," to Roosevelt's, "The only thing we have to fear is fear itself," to Groucho Marx's, "I don't care to belong to any club that will accept me as a member," to Lincoln's, "Fourscore and seven years ago," to Jefferson's, "We hold these truths to be self-evident," to Milton's, "Better to reign in hell than serve in heav'n," to Shakespeare's, "To be, or not to be, that is the question" — these lines are memorable not so much for *what* they say as *how* they say it — in other words, for their style. We remember them because they are pithy, clear, well-structured, to the point, and they sound good. While undoubtedly we preachers will not be composing lines fit for *Bartlett's Familiar Quotations*, we can seek to make each and every one of our own lines as memorable as possible by paying close attention to style.

> Great lines are memorable not so much for what they say as how they say it — in other words, for their style.

Our quest to create memorable sentences begins with the study of those lines that are fit for Bartlett's — the memorable sentences written by others. We learn not only by doing but by observing, and for a writer, the best teacher is a book. Reading great writing is an essential part of the preacher's continuing education. This is why I have often assigned fiction — short story collections — to beginning preaching classes, not to give them sources to mine for sermon illustrations, but as examples of the work of classic authors, the great communicators. As an ongoing practice, the preacher need not be limited to short stories, since superior style can be found in many forms: essays, novels, journalism, poetry. Even listening to talk radio can be a source of stylistic insight: how do people communicate when they have only their words to get the point across? The trick here is to choose the best possible models for our study; it will do us no good to go to a second- or third-rate writer to learn how best to put words together. Similarly, AM call-in radio may yield fewer insights about communication than the polished journalism of public radio. As with the selection of biblical commentaries and resources, the preacher will want to find reviews and exercise discernment. We wish to learn, whatever the source, but we learn best from the greats.

Attention to style will lend to our sermons two essential qualities: *recognition* and *identification*. These qualities are closely related. Recognition evokes the response, "I know that!" while identification evokes, "That's me!" Another way of saying this is that identification is personal recognition. Both are essential to the sermon, and both are created primarily by how we use language. We create recognition and identification by being specific; if I describe in detail a creature with pointy ears, fur, whiskers, and a purr, you will recognize a cat. If I describe your life to you — the kids are banging pots and pans in the kitchen, the Tylenol has yet to kick in, and your spouse is on the phone saying, "Honey, I'll be home late" *again* — then I will create identification. Recognition is talking about real things; identification is talking about real people. In both cases, we use language in order to create points of contact with our hearers. Recognition makes the sermon manageable for the hearer; the material presented is familiar, part of our daily life. Identification makes the material personal — "The preacher is talking to me!" Without recognition and identification, our sermons are mere abstract presentations of timeless truths, accurate enough but not life-changing — preaching that evokes a nod of the head, if we bother to think about it at all, but certainly not a transformed life. Without a style that invokes recognition and identification, we will never interest our hearers long enough for them to discover whether we have anything important to say.

> **Attention to style will lend to our sermons two essential qualities: recognition and identification. It will also make our sermons more memorable.**

The Oral Clock

The secret to style in the sermon — style that does create recognition and identification, that is generally memorable and interesting to listen to — is to write orally. To "write orally" should be recognized for the paradox it is — writing is not by nature oral, nor is speech writing. Yet we need to hold these opposites together for the sake of the sermon. The sermon itself is speech. Yet we will use writing in order to enable our speech. To accomplish that goal successfully, we must recognize that the conventions of writing are not the conventions of speech, and in order to make writing useful to our speaking, we must ignore or modify much of what we have learned about conventional writing, which is geared to looking good on the page, not sounding good when spoken. Paragraphs, for example, are for looking, not for hearing; we need them in written language, in order to group our material properly. In speaking, however, no one will see the paragraph breaks, so we will have to offer other cues to help our hearers arrange what they hear. We *are* going to write before we speak — writing is a necessary tool for most preachers, who need the focus and control that writing lends to the process of preparing a sermon (and if you can speak eloquently without writing anything down, you don't need this book!). Yet we are never going to write a word without the final product in view, which is not words on the page, but words spoken to our congregation. We will write in oral style, our words not to be seen, but heard.

The main difference between writing meant to be looked at and that meant to be heard has to do with time. Writing and speech work by different clocks — they live in different time zones. In written language, time is controlled by the reader. You can take as long as you want to read the words of this book. You can go back over the previous sentence and read it again. You can pause to think about something else, then skip over the next few paragraphs. If I make a mistake or compose a sentence poorly, you can spend extra time trying to figure out what looks wrong about it, or give up and put the book on a shelf. Time is under your control; I don't have any say about it, once I have put the words down on paper. You could read them now, next week, next year, or never, and there's nothing that I, the author, can do about it.

In a speech, however, we are in a different time zone entirely. The author, not the listener, controls the time. The listener has no control over time at all. The speech is delivered in the speaker's time, and at the speaker's rate. Am I speaking too fast for you to follow? Apart from jumping up and yelling at me to slow down, you have no control over time and pace. You cannot jump ahead to see the conclusion, because there is no conclusion to see — I will get to it when I get to it. If you pause to think about what I have said, you will miss the next thing. If you stare out the window and think about other things, a part of the speech will pass you by completely — you may never find your way back in. Time is totally in my control, and there is nothing that you, the hearer, can do about it, except go with the flow or tune out.

It follows that one of the key skills to develop in composing for oral delivery is the careful handling of time. This is a matter of style as much as delivery — we can and should, to some extent, vary our time of delivery according to the content of the sermon. But we need to compose our sermons with an eye to time, keeping in mind that we are controlling the time, not the hearer. Our main concern will be to provide the listeners with enough time to swallow what we have to say, but without giving them so much time that they end up looking out the window. We will have to exercise what I call a "controlled verbosity," a way of saying things that gives people time to get on board without making them bored. The more important the idea, the more unfamiliar the thought, the more time they will need. This is particularly true of transitions, when we are moving from one thought to another. We cannot expect people to adjust to a new thought quickly; they cannot see the paragraph break, nor the header. So we need to slow down at the point of transition. Where one sentence would do the trick in written language, the sermon must take two or three, all saying more or less the same thing. This redundancy, this "controlled verbosity," signals the transition, and gives the congregation time to make the mental adjustment to the new thought.

> Write in oral style, words not to be seen, but heard. In oral style, the author, not the listener, controls the time.

Thus, when I am writing something, I may make the following transition:

But speech does not function in the same way as written language.

The "But," along with the paragraph indentation, is your cue as a reader that I have made a contrasting transition. You can go back and reread the paragraph before, in order to refresh your mind about what I was saying before. If you're not clear about my new point, you can reread the sentence itself.

But if I am composing for oral presentation, none of those options will be present to you as the hearer. Time is entirely in my control now, and I will want to write accordingly, giving you a clear transition and time for your thought processes to adjust. I will write three sentences rather than one:

But we can't rely on visual cues when we write for speaking. Speech does not function in the same way as written language. There's nothing to see in a speech, only the speaker.

I have been redundant; I have said the same thing in three different ways. I have also given the hearer enough time to follow me into the next section. The use of "controlled verbosity" is an important tool for those who must write in order to speak.

But how do we know how it will sound to our hearers on Sunday morning? Quite simply, we can learn by creating their experience for ourselves beforehand. We can listen to the sermon in process with our ears, in order to anticipate what will happen to their ears. One of the most important things we can do in order to learn to write in oral style is to incorporate speaking into the composition from the beginning. The simple rule is, write the way you talk, not the way you write. I recommend composing aloud — speaking the words as you write them. It is when we actually hear words spoken that we notice the subtle differences between written and oral language. Certain things that we take for granted in writing sound stiff and unconvincing when spoken aloud. We will learn to ignore many of the "rules" pounded into us by our fourth-grade grammar teachers. We will split infinitives, if it sounds better that way ("To boldly go where no one has gone before"). We will not create clumsy sentences in order to avoid putting the preposition at the end of the sentence (a rule, said Winston Churchill, "up with which

> Oral writing cuts to the bone. Short words, short sentences. Easier to listen to, easier to remember.

I will not put!"). We will use contractions, where we would use them in ordinary speech. We may even use "incorrect" grammar and colorful, slangy vocabulary, if that is what the speech calls for (or we won't, if it ain't!). The only criterion we are going to apply is the oral one: does it sound good?

Our oral writing will cut to the bone. Short words, short sentences. Why? Short words and short sentences are easier to listen to. Also, the common vocabulary we all share tends to be made up of short words. If you have a choice, you will say, "telephone," instead of "wired communications," "dog," instead of "household pet." Seek an "A+ in school" not "excellence in learning objectives." Use the shortest word you can think of to describe something; this is not the time to impress people with your vocabulary, it is time to put things in their ears in such a way that they may be heard. Say "truth," not "veracity" or "verity." Say "love," not "amity" or "affection." Don't use a longer word where a shorter word will do, unless the longer word has just the needed nuance that the shorter one lacks; if you want to describe a transient sort of love, by all means say "infatuation" — if it is the shortest word with that precise meaning. Similarly, understand the differences in meaning between "aspiration" and "craving," "expectation" and "hankering," "yearning" and "anticipation" — but don't use any of the above when a simple "hope" will do. Above all, avoid jargon, especially the technical vocabulary of theology and biblical studies. The sermon is not the time to indoctrinate a congregation into TheoSpeak. The goal is to help people hear good news. Our vocabulary will match our purpose; it will be the common vocabulary that we use every day to communicate with everyone we meet. All the words we need for the sermon may be found in the daily newspaper.

As with our words, so with our sentences: oral sentences are to be short and sweet. Don't compose with quasi-Germanic grammar, making your hearers wade through qualification and subordinate clauses before they get to the main verb at the end — by that time, they may have forgotten what you were talking about! Long, convoluted sentences are to be broken into their component parts. Never leave the subject dangling far from the verb. Thus, the sentence below, while (marginally) acceptable for a written essay, will die a slow and torturous death in the ears of listeners:

The hearer — who is not accustomed to using theological vocabulary in the normal course of events, which for most people involves getting out of bed in the morning, eating breakfast, going to a job where a completely different technical vocabulary is used, one geared to the needs of the employer, not the employee, and certainly not the general public, where one can posit only an eighth-grade vocabulary level at best, due to the declining nature of public education — may not be able to understand, let alone appreciate, let alone remember, a complex verbal construction.

Put away your red pencil; this example isn't even worth editing. Cross it out and write this instead:

Hearers hear short best. The shorter, the better. They certainly won't understand jargon. Keep it short, sweet, and plain, using everyday words.

Another key to oral style — and another reason to speak aloud as we compose the sermon — is rhythm. When composing for oral presentation, we need to take into account the rhythm of the words and sentences we will use, both for ourselves and those we speak to. Words that trip lightly off our lips, teeth, and tongue will be easier for us to remember. They will also probably be memorable for the hearers. One can go into practically any church, order everyone to put the hymnals in the rack, and begin singing, "Amazing grace, how sweet the sound, that saved a wretch like me," and everyone will

> Incorporate speaking into composition from the beginning. Anticipate how it will sound.

begin to sing with you. It is not just the content that makes this hymn so memorable; the words fit perfectly with the simple yet striking melody. The rhythm of the sentence is a perfect match, and perfectly memorable. Try singing the words to a different tune, with a different rhythm — how long before you trip up on the words? (It so happens that the words can be sung to the tune of "Gilligan's Island" — I defy anyone to get through all the verses!). Some lines are memorable precisely because of their rhythm; in the example I used before, "To boldly go where no one has gone before," rendered without the split infinitive, would not be nearly so memorable, because the change would wreck the rhythm. We preachers are not primarily poets, nor are we writing for posterity (who knows what posterity will value, anyway?), but we can use rhythm to our advantage. If a sentence isn't working, is difficult to say or remember, or somehow doesn't quite sound right, try changing a few words around. The resulting rhythm may make all the difference.

The Rules

While we will be ignoring many of the conventional "rules" for written grammar (as it turns out, these are many of the same rules that good writers themselves ignore), we will be creating new rules of oral style for ourselves. Some of these rules also make for good written language. For example, in composing for oral presentation we will use active voice verbs, not passive. Active voice speaks directly and to the point. Passive voice evades and hides. Consider which you would rather hear:

Speak directly to be heard.

Or:

Speech that will be heard is to be put in active construction.

Active voice has the added virtue of being short and sweet, and thus doubly useful in oral composition. Count the words in:

The preacher read the manuscript poorly.

106

Compared to:

The sermon was delivered through a reading process by the preacher, who was ill-prepared.

Which will be easier to remember, when you rise to speak without a net on Sunday morning?

Perhaps the most important rule for oral style is to make maximum use of vivid verbs and concrete nouns. The words that are most memorable — and thus the easiest to speak and hear — are words that can evoke the senses, words that you can see, touch, taste, smell. They conjure something in the minds of those who hear them. The more vivid the verb, the more concrete the noun, the more likely a listener will create a picture, or smell a smell, or feel a texture. This is particularly important for oral style, precisely because the listeners cannot look at the page and see the words — they have nothing to grasp, unless the speaker gives it to them. Concrete nouns and vivid verbs are hooks for the listeners to hang on to.

Thus, preachers should take special care in the words they select. Here is another reason to avoid theological and religious jargon, most of which is abstract and uninspired. Instead, choose words that sing, that smell, that reach out and touch someone. Why simply "run," when you could "dart," "dash," "sprint," "trot," "scamper," or "skip"? You could walk into a "house," but the same street holds a "cottage," "duplex," or "brownstone," not to mention a "garage," a "barn," and a "shack." Don't just "look"; if necessary, "eye," "gaze," "stare," "gape," "peep," "scan," or even "scrutinize." Always choose the shortest and most appropriate word, yes — but make sure that the word you choose lives and breathes.

For example, think about how would you fill in the following sentence:

She _____ her farewell.

The uninspired choice would be "spoke," or perhaps, "waved." But what meanings could be conveyed simply by changing the verb, making it as vivid as possible: "She sang her farewell" or "She lilted her farewell" would mean something completely different from "She drooped her farewell" or even, "She spat her farewell." As an exercise, the preacher might want to take a simple sentence from last week's sermon, and see what range of meaning might result from the substitution of that tired old verb with something sparkling.

In the same way, preachers choose nouns that sparkle when they choose nouns that refer to real things and not abstractions. This is a prime factor in whether a sermon is able to hold and sustain the listeners' interest — does it talk about real life, or does it deal only in generalities? To talk about real life is to use concrete nouns, words that describe real things. It is to talk about "my dog Snoopy" instead of "our family pet," to speak of "plates and dishes and knives and forks" instead of "eating utensils," to talk about "Joe and Judy," real teenagers, instead of "kids these days." The sermon that invokes "love" will always get a nod if not a smile, but a sermon that speaks of "Romeo and Juliet" will get more. You can talk about "the power of prayer" all you want, but people will sit up and listen when you say, "We prayed with Joe at his bedside, the night he died." The difference is, where once you were speaking in abstract generalities, now you are talking about concrete and specific people and things. Evaluate every sentence of your sermon by this standard: have I used an abstract noun where a concrete one will do the same job? Make every sentence touch, taste, see, smell, hear. Do not write:

Politics is not the answer to our problem.

But instead:

The ballot box is not the answer to our problem.

Instead of:

Christianity is about compassion.

Try:

Christianity is one human hand reaching out to another.

The concrete noun is better than the abstraction, because it is easier to listen to, and easier to remember.

Making regular use of concrete nouns and vivid verbs helps us follow the next rule, which is to use adverbs and adjectives sparingly. Adverbs and adjectives, which modify nouns and verbs, also tend to weaken them. The way to make a noun stronger is not to modify it, but to change it to a strong, concrete noun that stands on its own. If our verb is colorless, we do not do it a favor by attaching an adverb to it; we actually make it worse. This is one of those rules that applies to written as well as oral communication, and a study of the great sentences of history bears it out. Shakespeare did not write, "To be, or not to be, that is the essential question." "Essential" would have been redundant, ruined the rhythm, and weakened the noun as well as the whole sentence. Roosevelt did not describe Pearl Harbor Day as "a day that will live forever in abject infamy," but simply as "a day that will live in infamy"; he did not need the adverb or the adjective. Similarly, the preacher may speak of "the grass," but need not speak of "the green grass," because we normally expect the grass to be green; if, however, we speak of "the brown grass," we are saying something else entirely. The test of an adverb or adjective is whether it is essential to the meaning of the sentence; if not, chances are it may

> Make maximum use of vivid verbs and concrete nouns. The words that are most memorable — and thus the easiest to speak and hear — are words that can evoke the senses, words that you can see, touch, taste, smell.

be dispensed with. If we choose concrete nouns and vivid verbs to begin with, we will not feel the need to spice the sentence with modifiers.

In using concrete nouns in particular, we will unavoidably be moving into the realm of metaphor and image. This is well and good, because able use of imagery can be a valuable skill for the preacher. Images are both concrete and memorable. In the example above, "the ballot box" is used as an image for "politics"; not only is it easily remembered, it has the advantage of being concrete, thus creating a picture in our minds. Often we preachers can substitute images for abstractions in our preaching; we do it quite naturally when, for example, we say "the cross" instead of "redemption" — thereby using short words, avoiding jargon, and creating a memorable picture. Similarly, we can speak of "a kiss" instead of "love," or "chains and padlocks" instead of "slavery." Generally speaking, any time you can substitute an image for an abstraction in a sermon, you should do it (or balance the abstraction with an image, so that one clearly interprets the other). The dangers of imagery and metaphor are two: that we overdo and mix the images, or that we fall into cliché. Mixed metaphors — where two or more images are placed in awkward conjunction — are common enough, even among good writers (the Apostle Paul was a notorious metaphor mixer), and usually result from an over-elaborated image. It is fine to take people over the bridge from the ancient world to the modern one, but I would avoid stopping off at too many islands along the way, lest your hearers miss the boat (!). Clichés are often images that have been burned so deeply into our ears that they have lost their power and seem trite. Preachers had best avoid them (like the plague!). Another way to deal with a cliché is to transform it, as in the description of the Middle-Eastern man who "knew which side his pita bread was buttered." A little creativity goes a long way.

Write specifically and directly, without unnecessary qualification, and without apology. Good style, written or oral, is direct and straightforward. Simply say what you think; don't say "maybe" or "probably" or "possibly" unless you have to — unless you mean it. Don't be afraid to use first person (singular or plural) where you mean it. Say "I" if you're talking about yourself; say "we" if you mean to include your hearers. Use "you" if you are talking about your audience but not yourself. A little honesty here will go a long way in the pulpit, because it will help us weed out our own preoccupations. Much of the "we" language in the pulpit is thinly-veiled "I" or "you" language — and the reason it has to be veiled is that it doesn't belong! "We" are not usually concerned with the season of the church year, or the difficulty of talking about a certain passage of Scripture; these are preacherly concerns, to which the congregation has given little or no thought before the preacher mentioned it. This sort of language is best left unspoken. Similarly, if the preacher says "we" are guilty of such-and-such a transgression, "we" had better be well-sure that "we" share that fault, and are not just sugarcoating a "you," because the congregation will easily see through such self-serving manipulation.

One way for preachers to increase the directness and specificity of their language is to avoid and/or replace pronouns, especially pronouns such as "this" and "that," "these" and "those." This is a consideration for oral as opposed to written style. Written language can make great use of pronouns, because the reader can always look back to see who "she" is, or what "that" refers to. In fact, written language is leaden without pronouns. But in spoken language, with time controlled not by the hearer but by the speaker, pronouns are often a liability. If the hearer misses the name in the first place, the identity of "she" will become an enigma. Better to repeat the name "Sue" once or twice than to have hearers wondering who "she" is. Demonstrative pronouns can be even more trouble, because in writing we often use "this" or "that" to refer back not to a specific thing but an entire sentence or complex of ideas: "We can conclude, because of this...." Here is an obvious instance where the speaker must substitute the idea, perhaps in concise form, in order to move the hearer along: "We can conclude, because of the nature of oral language...." In spoken language, "this" and "that," "these" and "those" are best used as pointing words — "this chair," "those apples" — rather than as stand-alone stand-ins for thoughts and ideas that the hearers may or may not have had time to catch.

Another way to increase the directness and specificity of our sermons is to avoid theological terms, or if we cannot avoid them, define them. We have already seen how theological jargon can hamper clear communication from the pulpit; our listeners have not been to seminary, and have probably not read any books on "process theology," "womanist ethics," or even "heilsgeschichte." Even familiar terms taken from Scripture may raise red flags. "Parousia" is Greek for "coming," and is often used as theological jargon for Christ's Second Coming — but how many people know that? The preacher should simply speak of "the Second Coming." Ditto for "Torah" instead of "Law," or "agape" instead of "love." Sermons should be in English, not Greek or Hebrew (or more accurately, sermons should be in the vernacular, the language of the people). Even words that are common enough in English and widely used in the churches may be unfamiliar or vague; how many people really understand the distinction between "justification" and "sanctification"? A word like "sin" is common enough, but most people do not use it in the Pauline sense of "the state of alienation from God" — otherwise it would make no sense to call chocolate cake a "sin." If we want to use the word "sin" to convey the Pauline sense, we are going to have to define it carefully. Such theological jargon is best left out of the pulpit and preserved for the classroom; this is advanced Christianity, not necessary for hearing the good news. Those who have taken the classes already know what you're talking about, and can appreciate the straightforward explanation in common language as much as the person who came in accidentally off the street.

The preacher will write according to purpose. Every sentence is to do clearly and concisely what it needs to do at that point in the sermon. Cicero and Augustine recognized this long ago when they spoke of "plain, middle, and grand" styles — intended respectively to inform, delight, and persuade. If we merely intend to convey information, we need to do that as clearly and concisely as possible, "Just the facts, ma'am." When we call directory assistance, we expect mere information, "The number is...." We don't want elaboration or verbal gymnastics; we have not called in search of a poem or a koan. Those portions of sermons that are meant to convey information should do exactly that and no more. But the sermon is more than just information, and so we will use other styles as appropriate. Sometimes we will wish to appeal to the emotions, to create a mood. Perhaps we will describe the rain dripping from a windowpane on a cold day, the drops almost but not quite freezing as they hit the glass. This is an appeal to the listener's sensibilities rather than an attempt to convey mere facts — we are trying to get under the skin. Once we do, we will then be able to convey those aspects of the gospel that have to do with feelings as much as facts — delight rather than information. Language intended to persuade will capitalize on the power of description. "People are starving in Africa" may get a nod of the head, but it won't compel your hearers to reach for their wallets. "Give generously" won't either. To compel their wills, you will have to touch their hearts, and this is what descriptive language is for: commercial appeals for famine relief on television show the babies with extended stomachs and spindly legs in order to touch us, and thus touch our wallets. We preachers, unless we wish to drag in a video screen, will have to accomplish our objective with nouns and verbs. The preacher has no pictures but those drawn with words.

This leads us to a fundamental rule of good style, oral or written: show, don't tell. Many of our previous observations fall under this one basic rule; for example, when we are using concrete nouns in place of abstractions, we are showing rather than telling. But the axiom does not apply just to images and stories — all parts of our composition need to show rather than simply tell. An argument is not made by simply stating the conclusion; that is telling. To show the argument is to spell out all the steps one-by-one, giving examples, so that our hearers will follow along and agree with our conclusion. Our sermons will not touch the mind, heart, and will if we merely state such-and-such to be the case, but only if we actually make it the case. Our words have to create the reality we describe. Showing, not telling, will make our sermons memorable. We wish to say something that is easily heard as well as easily recalled. So we do not merely tell; we show.

A significant rule for one who would show not tell is this: talk about real people. This is often the difference between a sermon that evokes merely a nod of the head and one that reaches the hearts and wills of the listeners. Many preachers speak of every-

> Show, don't tell. Talk about real people.

thing but real people — perhaps we talk about the biblical characters a bit, and maybe if we're lucky we'll have a personal reference or two — but the rest of the sermon is filled with that vague "we" who is everyone and no one, an ideal construct that applies to no real person, a shadow who is constantly struggling with and affirming the abstractions of the Christian faith, but never actually gets down to the reality of Christian life. The sermon swims in a sea of abstractions, because it never bothers to ask what difference this abstract content might make to a flesh-and-blood human being. Subjected to a lifetime diet of such sermons, one might be tempted to agree with Homer Simpson: "Christianity? Oh, yeah, that religion with the nice rules that don't work."

Tell Me A Story

If we are going to show, not tell about, real people in the sermon, we are going to tell stories. Story is a topic that often sheds as much smoke as light on the preaching process. Some homileticians swear by story, going so far as to insist that the sermon must be structured like a story, or must contain nothing but stories. Some even contend that the Bible or Christianity itself is little more than a story. Other homileticians decry the story-sermon and even the use of stories in sermons, holding that they distract from the communication of the gospel. While we have neither the time nor the place to examine the issue in full — our purpose is to learn to compose in a memorable oral style, not to solve an academic debate — it is safe to say that neither extreme holds exclusive claim to the truth. Stories are indeed one of the most powerful tools in the preacher's arsenal. And it is precisely because they are so powerful that they can be so dangerous.

Stories to be used in sermons must be carefully prepared; this is not the time to ad-lib, even for one who would preach without a net. This is because we want the story to serve our ultimate purpose, which is the proclamation of the good news. Stories can help us do that, but because they are so powerful, they can sometimes take over the sermon in ways we did not intend. Because they are so memorable, we preachers may be tempted to ride them further than our intended stopping point, and thus let the story take over the sermon rather than be its servant.

Careful trimming of our stories is essential to making them serve our purposes. For each story, ask, "What is the purpose here?" Is this story an illustration of a point? If so, what point? Or is the story itself the point? Once we have determined the purpose of the story, we can trim it accordingly. Many stories in sermons are over-elaborated; they contain material that does not serve the purpose of the story. If your story is about a sign on the side of a barn in Tennessee, your congregation does not need to know why you were in Tennessee, what kind of car you were driving, or who was with you. Such personal items will be more of a distraction than a help to the story. Your congregation will end up thinking about you, not your point. But, you say, the personal details are what make the story come alive! Think about it: if the story isn't very interesting without the personal material, that should tell you something. And even non-personal material is sometimes superfluous. If the point is what the sign said, it may not make any difference that it was in Tennessee. The story in this case should begin, "I once saw a sign on the side of a barn...."

Stories should also be told from a single point of view. If it is about what you saw on the side of the barn, stick to your point of view. If it makes a difference what your kids saw on the barn, that's another story. Rarely can a story make a successful shift from one point of view to another; if you begin describing Zacchaeus' view from the top of the tree, it won't do to switch to Jesus' perspective later. This is because as the preacher, you are one character, not many. Excepting the skilled actor, one person cannot play several roles at once, or even in succession. Be Jesus, or be Zacchaeus, but don't try to move back and forth.

The beginner may wonder where all these sermon stories are going to come from. How could I possibly come up with even one story per week, let alone two or three? There is no magic here. The sources of stories for the sermon are many. We have already mentioned a prime source, Scripture itself. We may lament biblical illiteracy in the congregation, but how will they know the stories we never tell them? Our outside reading will often provide us with stories for sermons; literature is a prime source of stories that are already memorable and well-told. Nonfiction memoir and biography can also provide stories. The preacher's personal experience can be a prime source of stories for the sermon, if used discretely (see below). Television and film are also important sources for stories that will create recognition and identification in our hearers. While some may wonder whether so-called "pop" culture is appropriate sermon material (if culture represents the most common facets and trends of a people, is there any culture other than "pop" culture?). The answer is quite simply that if you want to reach the majority of modern human beings, you will have to speak in a familiar language. Pretending that your congregation does not watch television or read the funny pages simply will not do. This is particularly true for those younger folks we church people so often claim to worry about. In an age that values resistance to authority and skepticism about truth claims, we cannot expect to speak in a theological ghetto and gain a hearing from those who live on Main Street. Perhaps in the hands of preachers of questionable taste, modern culture can be made to trivialize faith (as Deacon Dolson complained in the play *Mass Appeal,* "I grew up thinking Snoopy was one of the twelve apostles"). But one can be relevant without being trivial. If we ignore the modern media, we run the risk not only be being irrelevant, but of missing some bitingly useful stuff. Some of the most piercing social and theological commentary in the last decade has come not from any preacher or essayist or social critic, but from the animated characters of *The Simpsons.*

Our use of stories is governed not only by their fit in the sermon, but by a sense of ethics. We will not, for example, pretend that fictional stories actually happened to us (unless we offer some clues that they are in fact fictional). This is especially true for stories we gain from common sources, like newspapers or preaching

116

aids. Nothing is more embarrassing than hearing a preacher tell of his dramatic rescue from a cave, then hearing the same story in the same words from some other preacher. Even if our story comes from our own lives, we will want to exercise a certain caution. We will never divulge pastoral confidences, even from past churches (what, you want to signal everyone in the pews that anything they tell you may be blurted out in some future parish?). We will be very careful about telling personal stories about our friends and families without their permission. And we will be very, very careful lest we become the implicit subject of our own stories, so that rather than helping proclaim the gospel, the story ends up proclaiming ourselves. The congregation may perk up its ears when you talk about yourself, but often the result is that they hear more about you personally than the gospel. When in doubt, personal stories can be cast in the third person, so they offer less of a distraction: "I know someone who once...."

Beginning preachers often wonder whether they should cite the sources of their stories or other quoted material. While it is essential that you acknowledge someone else's material (especially a direct quote), usually less is more. In normal conversation we do not say things like, "Walker Percy, a great southern novelist, once said...." And it seems awkward to spend a whole sentence footnoting your source: "Walker Percy was a great southern novelist. He once said...." Unless it makes a difference that Walker Percy said it, or that he was southern, or that he was a novelist, the preacher can probably get by with a more generic attribution: "Someone once said...." This has the merit of being concise, unobtrusive, and not telling more than was needed. If there is some reason we need to know about Walker Percy, however, by all means put him in there. The same could be said for both famous people and famous sayings; most people will recognize the sailor John Paul Jones as the one who said, "I have not yet begun to fight," so it would be silly to say that "someone" once said it. Likewise, most people know who the Pope is, or who the President is, or who Bill Gates is. One might only note that fame is fleeting, and our assumptions about fame may show our age; while many people know who Howard Cosell was, not many of them are under thirty.

Paper

Our process has brought us to the actual point of sermon composition. We have studied Life, we have studied the Scriptures. We have brainstormed the connections between Life and Scripture. We have summed up our thinking in a theme sentence. We have chosen a structure, and we probably have a good idea of some of the language that will appear in the sermon itself. Or quite honestly, perhaps we do not. We sit down with a prayer and hope that the Spirit will inspire us once we get going. At any rate, we are now ready to write something.

As I have already noted, we will use paper and ink (or the computer keyboard, as the case may be) in several different ways during the entire process of creating a sermon. We take notes on our study, we scribble during brainstorming, and now we write a preliminary draft of what we will say on Sunday (our next step, covered in the following chapter, is revision/rehearsal — we revise the draft sermon while we rehearse its delivery). We do a lot of writing as we prepare for Sunday. Our goal, however, is to speak, so what we write now must serve our eventual speaking. If we are able, we will speak the words aloud as we compose them. Some preachers find this too laborious a process, as the words do not come out of the fingers at the same rate they come out of the mouth. If you do not speak aloud as you compose, the process of refining the words orally can wait for later — but it may well add an extra step to your work.

Why write at all, if we are going to speak in the end? The issue for one who would preach without a net is control versus freedom. Having a written draft of the sermon offers us maximum control — we can put this word precisely there, we can move this section before that, we can tell the story this way or that way, at the beginning, middle, or end. We can go through our manuscript and ruthlessly slice the jargon, the convoluted sentences, the passive voice verbs, the lifeless abstractions, and the ambiguous pronouns. Writing gives us maximum control over the composition process in a way that, for example, speaking into a tape recorder does not. As we will see, writing also gives the preacher visual cues — something to hang on to, to look at, as we go through the process of revision/rehearsal. In the end, however, we are going to free ourselves from the need for this much control. The process of revision/rehearsal will loosen us from the original manuscript, and give us the freedom to sound spontaneous. In the end, the manuscript will be a guideline that we have internalized, a route drawn on a map and drilled into our brains. When we're actually on the highway, we're free to drive, but we know where we're going and all the stops along the way. Beginning sermon composition with a written

> Our goal is to speak. What we write must serve our speaking. Use an oral manuscript form.

manuscript offers us maximum control; learning to leave the manuscript behind us allows us the freedom to sound spontaneous.

It is important to recognize that what we are writing here is only the first draft. It is *not* the sermon, but only a starting point for the process of revision/rehearsal, which will eventually lead to delivery. Our writing is always in service of the end product, which is our speaking. We sit down to write the first draft, but our minds put us in the pulpit as we write. We see ourselves speaking the words, clearly, comfortably, with confidence and without hesitation. The first draft is actually the first step of the process of revision/rehearsal.

While there is much to keep in mind as you compose your first draft — everything we have covered so far in this chapter, to be precise — there is one thing to keep in the foreground: *be memorable.* I cannot repeat it too often: the key to preaching without a net is to compose something memorable. If we are going to say it without notes or manuscript, we must write memorably. We will have to remember it ourselves, in order to preach it, and it will be easier for us to remember in the end if we begin by writing something worth remembering. The first step in our own memory process is simply to write the best sermon we are capable of, week after week. As I've said before, this means taking the time to get it right. To preach without a net is no shortcut process. It is hard work. But it is worth it, not only because we will develop in our

This is the oral manuscript form.
  It is organized by thought-units, not paragraphs.
  Paragraphs are a written convention, and cannot be seen
    when you speak.
  The oral manuscript form is meant to give the preacher
    visual cues as to how the sermon is organized.
  Each sentence goes on a separate line. Actually, you can
    group a couple of short sentences on one line, if they
    are closely connected.
  Every line is given a hanging indentation.
    A sub-thought may be indented further, if necessary.
  Having each sentence or group of sentences on a separate
    line makes the lines easier to remember than if they
    are in paragraphs.
    It also provides a transitional advantage: because of
      the line-by-line format, this manuscript form can
      be easily read from the pulpit by those who are
      not quite ready to preach completely without a
      net.

To start a new thought-unit, double-space and begin at the
  margin.
  Indent the next line to continue the thought-unit.
  Etc.

Figure 3

own preaching abilities, but because we will be offering to God
and to our congregations something memorable.

Since we will be writing with our final goal, speaking, in view,
I suggest an approach to writing that keeps that goal in sight. I put
my first drafts in what I call an "oral manuscript form" (see Fig.
3). I do not use the paragraphs of conventional writing — remember, no one can see the paragraphs of speech, they are strictly written conventions. Instead, I group my writing according to "thought-
units," consisting of indented thoughts and sub-thoughts, listed

line-by-line. Every sentence, or group of closely-related sentences, goes on a separate line. The sentences are given hanging indentation, to show their relationship to what comes before and after. When I have finished a thought-unit, I double space and go to the margin to start a new one. The advantage of the oral manuscript form over conventional paragraphs is clear. Every sentence begins on a new line, with the white space indicating its relationship to the entire thought-unit. I can tell at a glance how this sentence fits into the whole. It is also clear whether the sentence is the short, sweet oral writing I prefer — if it takes more than a line or two, it's not! The manuscript form as a whole gives me visual cues that I will make use of in the revision/rehearsal process — this sermon has six thought units, I see from looking over the manuscript, and the first one has seven lines. The form also has advantages for those who would like to learn to preach more spontaneously, but are not quite ready to do entirely without a net. Put your oral manuscript in a suitably large typeface, and take it into the pulpit with you — you'll never lose your place, because each sentence starts on a line of its own, with clear indication of what comes before and after. Once you've tried an oral manuscript form, you'll never go back to paragraphs.

When we have composed the first draft of the sermon, we have already taken a step into the next stage of the sermon process — we have begun the process of revision/rehearsal, which will take us to Sunday and delivery without a net. We are not quite ready to walk the tightrope, since our training is not yet complete — but Sunday is coming, soon and very soon. We are only a day or two away.

Stand And Speak

In a nutshell: Delivery relies on memory, and memory is enhanced by an active process of rehearsal and revision that internalizes the composition until we know it by heart. We learn our sermons as actors learn their lines, but unlike most actors, we have the freedom to improve our lines as we rehearse, and even as we deliver the sermon.

We are coming to the end of the week — Friday, if not Saturday. Our week has been spent working through the acts of rhetoric. We first engaged in study (what Cicero called *invention*) that determined the content of the sermon, and resulted in a single pithy statement of what the sermon was to be about (the "theme sentence"). The theme sentence became the first act of the next step, which was composition of the first draft of the sermon, in which we paid careful attention to the sermon's form, both structure and language (Cicero's *arrangement* and *style*). Sunday is coming — soon we must stand and speak — so we now consider the final acts of rhetoric, *memory* and *delivery*.

Memory and delivery are separate but one. They are to be considered together as two aspects of the same thing (just as structure and language taken together constitute form). The obvious reason, for one who would preach without a net, is that nothing can be delivered that is not remembered. All the hard work in the study, all the effort of putting words down on the page (in short, all the work we did this week), will be for nothing if we cannot remember any of it — unless of course we take our paper with us into the pulpit. But this is what we are trying to avoid. We have entered into this discipline because we would like to preach in a more spontaneous style that does not rely on reading manuscripts from the pulpit on Sunday morning. If we are tempted to throw the towel in on Saturday — what the hey, the manuscript's done, it won't get any better between now and then, might as well read it tomorrow and watch the game this afternoon — we need only recall the vacant stares of boredom we saw last week every time we looked up from our monotone. We have ventured down this road — the one less traveled, to be sure — because we are convinced that our preaching need not be shallow nor boring, and that developing a spontaneous delivery style is a worthy goal for ourselves and a suitable gift for those who bothered to get up early on Sunday morning to come hear us speak. This is no time to turn back. We would preach without the net of a sermon manuscript, so we must rely on memory for our delivery. For our purposes, memory and delivery are one.

But memory is also the bridge between composition and delivery. It must be so if we are to preach without a net. Our memory process will not be passive but active, and involve a continuous reconsideration of composition in light of delivery. The simple truth is that we cannot deliver that which does not lend itself to being delivered. Our first draft will be in need of revision, according to the dictates of delivery. This revision is thus a sort of rehearsal as well (and we can consider revision/rehearsal to be one thing). The act of memory takes place as we lead ourselves through the process of revision and rehearsal toward delivery. Memory is buttressed by revision and rehearsal that internalizes our composition, until we know our sermon by heart.

Revision/Rehearsal, Learning By Heart

Of course we must revise. Rare is the writer who will get every word right the first time (and the one who thinks so probably gets into fights with editors, or is never published). Writing is rewriting. The first draft of sermon composition is thrown together, words put down in the heat of the moment under the throes of inspiration. We thank God for the inspiration (if not the throes), and capitalize on it as best we can. But this is not to say that reflection will not improve the original — does this word belong here, that theme there? Do subjects, verbs, and tenses match? Is the tone consistent? Everything should be weighed in the clear light of day. It is perhaps best if the preacher take a break after the composition of the first draft — to take a day before returning to it, if possible, or at least to take a break before lunch.

The process of revision is necessary to refine our sermon draft. But the standard for our revision is not words on the page, but the words to be spoken on Sunday morning. Our final goal is the sermon itself, and never has it been so important to keep this in mind as in the process of revising the first draft. Revision must have a future orientation, which means an oral orientation. Quite simply, we revise according to how the words sound.

> Nothing can be delivered that is not remembered. If you can't remember it, you probably need to revise it.

Thus, the revision process is also a rehearsal process. The only way we can adequately assess our written words is to speak them aloud. The most effective way to speak them is to imagine ourselves actually preaching them. The revision/rehearsal process is an imaginative exercise, in which we judge for ourselves how effectively our words will communicate on Sunday morning. The flaws in our written words will become obvious once we utter them in an imaginary preaching moment — the long sentences will seem awkward, the abstractions lifeless, the difficult words and phrases will become tongue-twisters. Even if we did not wish to preach entirely without a written manuscript in the pulpit, we could greatly improve our preaching by this simple exercise. Revision/rehearsal helps us turn the written draft into words that can be easily spoken on Sunday morning.

Revision/rehearsal is also a memory aid. The more times we run through the draft sermon, the more familiar it will seem. The awkward, unmemorable passages will smooth out in the process of revision, and because we have revised them, we will remember them. Again, many a manuscript preacher would find great improvement simply by engaging in an hour of revision/rehearsal on Saturday afternoon. Some preachers think that the sermon is "done" once they have composed a written manuscript. But on Sunday, they take the manuscript into the pulpit and find the words odd and unfamiliar — it might as well have been written last month. A little time spent revising it, in the process of imagining the delivery, would have made the manuscript into a friend rather than a stranger. But why not go further? If we are going to take the time to revise and rehearse, we might as well go the next step, and dispense with the manuscript (read on to see exactly how to do this). If we can remember the words we have composed, we don't need the paper. The trick is to see the process of composition as a fluid one that leads through memory via revision/rehearsal to delivery itself. For one who would preach without a net, the sermon is never done until it is preached.

One way to think about delivery, in fact, is simply as an extension of the revision/rehearsal process. Our goal is to develop a spontaneous-sounding style, even though we have begun by writing down every word. We do not treat those written words as sacred — they are all subject to the process of revision. We revise them according to how well we can speak them. Soon we will find ourselves making spontaneous revisions as we speak — a noun here, a verb there, a grammar tweak there. The process of revision/rehearsal will become so natural to us that we will think nothing of making this kind of change even in the pulpit on Sunday morning. We make the revision in the final version, perhaps because it only just occurred to us — the inspiration required a night's sleep, and came to consciousness only when we arrived at the proper point. We can revise on the fly because such revision is of one piece with the process we have been following. Revision/rehearsal teaches us to balance control and freedom; the written draft gave us control over our words, so that we knew exactly what we were going to say, but we also learned freedom as we practiced the words and changed them in the practicing. We have rehearsed revising. Thus we sound spontaneous, without actually speaking off-the-cuff.

As a practical matter, I do my revision/rehearsal with the first draft before me on paper, with pen or pencil in hand. Though I write the first draft on computer, revising on the keyboard seems to make the revision/rehearsal process more complicated than need be. Also, printing out the draft allows me to do my revision/rehearsal away from the computer desk. So I do my revisions on paper, and record the results for posterity on the computer later. Before printing the draft copy that I will use for revisions, I reduce the typeface and spacing so that the entire sermon

> Final delivery is an extension of the revision/rehearsal process. The sermon is never done until it is preached, and even as it is preached, it is in the final stages of composition.

fits on two pages. This allows me to look at the entire sermon at one glance, as it is all laid out in front of me on two pieces of paper (and later, when I print a file copy, I'll do the same, so that the whole sermon will fit on one piece of paper, front and back — saving a lot of space in the file cabinet). The usual length of my sermons allows me to do this without scrunching up the type so much that it is unreadable; those with longer sermons may find they need three pages, which can still be laid out on a desk for a bird's-eye view. I do this because I want to be able to get a sense of the entire sermon at once as I work on it — opening, ending, and everything in-between, all in one swoop. On Sunday, we must remember not only the individual words, one after another, but how the entire structure holds together. My revision/rehearsal manuscript thus serves the process of memory and delivery.

Since the revision process is also a rehearsal process, even at the earliest stages, the preacher should be imagining and actually experiencing the final delivery. Picture yourself standing in your usual preaching place. Imagine the light, the textures, the faces of the people you will be looking at. This will help you from becoming fixated on the pages in front of you — remember, they are not the sermon, but merely tools that will help you deliver the sermon on Sunday. Begin by looking up from the page as you mouth the words written there — not only will it help you to get an experience of what the sermon will be like, but it will aid your memory — from the beginning, you are speaking, not reading! Some preachers find it best to do their revision/rehearsal in front of a mirror, in order to simulate eye contact. Don't speak unless you're looking at yourself in the mirror; if you need to look down for the next line, do so, but look up again to say it. After going through the sermon several times in this manner, you will find yourself looking more and more in the mirror, and less and less at the pages. In fact, this may be the only memory work you need to do before Sunday — if you can get through the whole sermon without taking your eyes off the mirror to look down at the page, you are ready to go!

In the revision/rehearsal process, the experience is everything. It is not just a matter of choosing the proper words, or of saying them so many times that they are drilled into our brains. The sermon must have integrity. There must be an emotional congruence between the message and the messenger. You cannot preach that which you do not believe — that which you cannot give your heart to. In the revision/rehearsal process, we will be putting our whole beings — body, heart, and soul — into what will be the sermon. This is one of the things that makes it memorable; we don't just think about it, we feel it. Like the pianist who plays from memory, the music is in our fingers. By Sunday morning, the sermon is in us, waiting to get out.

Some of us, however, find that the process of revision/rehearsal as outlined so far is not enough to carry us all the way to the pulpit on Sunday morning. We know a good deal of the sermon, yes, but we can't get all the way through it without looking down at the page. We can't walk away from the paper and say the whole thing. Sometimes the problem is that we need more revision — this sentence here does not quite lend itself to being spoken, perhaps if I change the word-order — but it may well be that we have done all the revising we can do for now. We have done revision/rehearsal, but we are not ready to preach without a net. We must go on to the next step in the act of memory, which is learning the sermon by heart.

Note that I say "learn by heart," and not "memorize." Learning by heart is an extension of the revision/rehearsal process, not rote memorization of cold facts. It involves not just our minds, but our whole beings. As we have seen, preaching must invoke our hearts and wills as well as our minds, our bodies and well as our souls, and the revision/rehearsal process takes that into account by forcing us to imagine ourselves in the preaching moment as we prepare for it. It is a short step from that continual re-experiencing of the sermon to the complete internalization of the words so that they will flow naturally from us. Learning our sermon by heart is the last step of revision/rehearsal before delivery.

> It is a short step from the continual re-experiencing of the sermon to the complete internalization of the words. Learning the sermon by heart is the last step of revision/rehearsal.

Some preachers may object at this point that "learning by heart" still sounds like "memorizing every word of the sermon." Indeed, it will probably come to that, for most of us who prepare manuscripts in order to preach. I certainly would not stand to preach unless I knew exactly what I had planned to say. The plan I am proposing is a way of making the words easy to remember, not avoiding the need to remember them. If we were the kind of preachers who are naturally skilled at composing sermons on the fly, we would not need this discipline. Recall why we need to compose a manuscript in the first place: we aren't very good on our feet, and we need the control over content, language, and structure that writing a manuscript brings. It stands to reason that before we stand to preach, we need to learn the words of the manuscript, in order to preserve that control. Further, we need such control in order to find the freedom of a spontaneous delivery. Ironically, spontaneity is found only when we have mastered our material — only when we know what we want to say can we effectively improvise on it. We will not have the freedom we seek, until we have learned our lines.

It is at this point that preaching is best compared to acting. Some may rightly resist the comparison, since "acting" implies not only entertainment but fakery — and while we preachers want to be interesting, we may cringe if someone calls us "entertaining," and get downright hostile if accused of fakery. But we should not think of preaching as any old kind of acting; I would compare it to one approach in particular, "Method" acting. The "Method" describes an approach to acting that tries to incorporate an imaginative approach to experience into the acting moment, and is best illustrated by the (perhaps apocryphal) story about an exchange between Dustin Hoffman and Laurence Olivier during the filming of *The Marathon Man*. Hoffman, a Method actor and title character, did a little running to get into the spirit of his role. Sweaty, huffing and puffing, he ran up to Olivier and said, "Boy, this is a tough role." Olivier, who had classical, Shakespearian training, arched an eyebrow and said, "Have you ever tried *acting*?" We preachers want to be Hoffman rather than Olivier, runners rather than merely actors. We want to experience the sermon as we rehearse it, because the very subject matter requires us to. We want to learn the sermon by heart, rather than memorize it. We won't try acting. We will follow the Method. We are not going to fake it, but live it.

How will we learn our sermons by heart? The same way actors do — one line at a time. Again, this is simply an extension of the revision/rehearsal process. Read a line, look up, and say it. If you can get all the way through it, read the next line. Look up, and say both lines together. Proceed in this manner with the next line, and the next, until you can get all the way through a thought-unit, and then begin with the next thought-unit. When you have two thought-units learned, say them together. Move through the sermon this way, until you can say the whole thing by heart. Revise along the way if the Spirit moves; you are preparing to speak on Sunday morning, when you will know exactly what you want to say, but you will have freedom to change it as needed.

130

One trick I have found helpful in learning a sermon by heart is to start from the back and work to the front. Begin with the first line of the final thought-unit, and continue to the end. Then take the previous thought-unit, learn it, and go through both together. Keep working in this way backwards to the front of the manuscript. I don't know exactly why this works as well as it does — perhaps it is because I spend the greatest emotional energy composing the beginning of a sermon, so that the ending is least familiar, and this process adds equilibrium. Starting to learn by heart from the rear will ensure that your ending is the most familiar part of your sermon on Sunday morning, because it has been rehearsed the most. There is something to be said for knowing your sermon backwards and forwards.

> Learn the sermon by heart line-by-line, one thought-unit at a time, from the back to the front.

The beginner may worry that this revision/rehearsal process, culminating in learning the sermon by heart, will take more preparation time than one actually has on Saturday afternoon. It is true that at first, you are going to have to be quite intentional about leaving enough time to prepare for Sunday. But eventually this process will become a habit and seem the most natural thing in the world — and as a habit, will take less time than you think. I usually divide my revision/rehearsal time into two segments. The first is a period of about an hour and half that is devoted mainly to the revision side of things — this is the time I whip the draft sermon into what will be more or less the final form. Sometimes the sermon is ready to be preached by the end of this period. More likely, I take a break and come back later to spend about an hour learning the lines by heart. Before I go to bed Saturday night, the sermon is ready to go. I am quite confident that I will not need a net under the pulpit the next morning.

The preacher will have to find both time and place for uninterrupted revision/rehearsal. While some preachers actually go into the church and climb the pulpit to rehearse for Sunday, I find I need more seclusion for this work — the sermon is not quite ready to be heard by others, and you never know who is going to wander into the church. The open space of the church is too vulnerable at this stage. I find it best to go into an office or bedroom — somewhere that will not be busy with foot traffic — shut the door, and turn off the phone ringer. On Sunday mornings, I usually rehearse my sermon one last time alone in the shower, or in the car on the way to church. Others may plan their revision/rehearsal time differently. One preacher's practice may or may not be helpful to you, as you find your own work pattern. Maybe the rhythm of your family life is such that sermon composition, revision and rehearsal must be finished and out of the way by Friday afternoon. The important thing is to find a time and a place that works for you. This uninterrupted revision/rehearsal time must be observed as intentionally as the time set aside for study and composition, however. While there is always the possibility that an emergency may interrupt the process, true emergencies are relatively rare; most things can wait an hour and a half. Keep in mind your priorities — what is so important that it takes precedence over the responsibility of delivering the Word of God to your congregation?

Stand And Speak

For many preachers who work from a written manuscript, the process of revision/rehearsal described here is a major change in their manner of working. Those blessed with the gift of gab may be able to step into the pulpit without their written manuscript, or without the few notes they jotted down on a sheet of yellow legal paper, but for most of us, the thought of ascending the pulpit with no paper at all really is like stepping out on a tightrope without a net below to catch us if we fall. While the metaphor is not quite apt (we will not die if we fall from the pulpit, or even break a bone) forgetting what we were going to say in the pulpit on Sunday may well make us wish we were dead! This is what keeps preachers bound to their manuscripts; better to be boring, than to die of embarrassment.

It is therefore important for most of us to take baby steps as we learn to preach without a net. Start small, and move cautiously.

This week, work through your manuscript as usual, then spend some time in revision/rehearsal. Take the manuscript into the pulpit with you, and see how you do. I imagine that you will find that you need the manuscript less than last week. Try this for a couple of weeks, and soon you may find that the manuscript gets in your way rather than helps. You are now ready to preach without a net.

Another approach would be to pick small sections of the sermon and resolve to preach that section — and only that section — without referring to your manuscript. Pick a story first, since stories are easily remembered. Preach your sermon as before, but when it comes time for the story, look up at your audience and keep your eyes there. Let the story come. Next week, pick another part of the sermon, the thought-unit that covers the argument from Scripture, perhaps. Gradually build up your confidence so that you can do two or three thought-units each week without referring to your manuscript. People will begin to tell you that they notice something different about these parts of your sermon; what is happening is that they can tell the difference between your fully oral delivery and the parts you read from the manuscript. Continue the process until you can preach most if not all your manuscript without looking; you soon won't need the manuscript at all. You have taken a few steps out on the tightrope, then hurried back, then a few more, hurried back, and a few more, until you are halfway across and there's no reason not to go forward rather than backward. Time to take down the net.

> Take baby steps as you learn to preach without a net. Gradually work yourself up to using no paper at all on Sunday mornings.

There may also be transitional points between taking a full manuscript into the pulpit and taking no paper at all — a graduated approach to the paperless pulpit. Perhaps you will want to distill parts of your manuscript into notes, so that you must rely on memory. The manuscript you take with you on Sunday will be complete at certain points, but at others it will merely say, "Tell the story about Uncle Al," or "Explain how the Corinthians thought about this," and this line will remind you of a section that you took

133

special pains to learn by heart. When you are feeling comfortable doing one section in every sermon from only the prompt, try doing two or three. Once you get to the point where you are ready to do the entire sermon this way, your manuscript will consist of nothing but prompts. Another way to do this is to use a manuscript that contains nothing but the first line of each thought-unit. Once you have been reminded of the first line, the rest of the thought unit should come flowing out. If it doesn't, you're not entirely without a net; you can always look down and go to the next thought unit.

Gaining gradual freedom from the tyranny of the manuscript will enable the preacher to gain a greater awareness of what is happening in the moment of sermon delivery. You are, in the words of a well-known homiletician, "doing time in the pulpit." The sermon is an event in time and space. Something is happening here in real life. You can look out and see the effects of your words on the hearers. Some have their eyes fixed on you; some are distracted by the people in the next pew; some seem lulled into their own worlds, and you can't tell if they're listening or not. They are not just hearers; they are watching. They are assessing you, to see if your mouth lies while your twitching fingers tell the truth, to see if there is conviction in your eyes or merely resignation, or perhaps confusion. As the preacher, you give them space to hear and see, time to think or not think. There is a dynamic going on here that you could only half pay attention to, when you were reading off a manuscript.

Being in the moment of the sermon delivery, rather than wrapped up in the words of a sermon manuscript, will provide a lot of feedback about sermon composition. Do they laugh at the jokes? If not, maybe they are not funny, or not appropriate. Do they fall asleep during the scriptural exposition, but wake up for the story about Uncle Al? Perhaps next week you'll want to give the language of your scriptural exposition all the vivacity of the words that described Uncle Al. Preaching without a net means coming to grips with audience participation — are they there with you, or not, and if not, what aspect of sermon composition is at fault?

Freedom from manuscripts also allows the preacher to pay attention to the mechanics of delivery. A primary quest for the beginning preacher is finding one's natural pulpit voice. We may think that our pulpit voice is simply our natural conversational voice, but we would be wrong. The voice we can use to talk to one or two people standing two feet away from us will never be adequate to fill a room full of a hundred people. Unfortunately, some of us adopt a phoney-sounding "preacher's voice" that includes a singsong cadence and odd pronunciations, and is quite at odds with the modern conversational standards of eloquence. The trick here is to find ways to sound conversational that nevertheless project to the entire crowd. Proper vocal production is essential.

> Use the freedom of preaching without paper to improve your composition and delivery.

Vocal production begins with breath support. We exhale when we speak, so our speaking depends on muscle control — we must be able to control the wind expelled from our lungs. This is why we speak of breath "coming from the diaphragm" — it really comes from the lungs, of course, but proper control is enabled by the diaphragm, a large horizontal muscle that acts as a bellows, pushing air in and out of the lungs. To breathe "from the diaphragm" is to gain consciousness of how this muscle can help us control our exhalation, and thus our speech. Any singer will tell you that the first step in learning to feel our diaphragm is to lie down on the floor and breathe — your shoulders cannot move, so you will feel and see the movement as you breathe in and out (technically, we do not move the diaphragm itself, but the abdominal muscles that control it). When we stand and begin to take the same kind of breath, we will be able to take longer and deeper breaths, and thus be able to speak with more powerful, deeper, and richer voices.

As your breath is exhaled from the lungs, it acquires pitch from the vocal cords, and resonance as it passes through a series of amplifiers: the throat, nose, and sinus cavities. This is what allows you to project your voice to be heard throughout the room, and also gives your voice color. It is usually easy to recognize problems with resonance — too much nasal resonance gives you that "twang" sound, while tension in the throat produces stridency. Such resonance problems can usually be cured by relaxation exercises and proper breath support.

The final stage of speech is articulation, which is produced by mouth, tongue, and teeth. This is what shapes the wind into vowels and consonants, words and sentences. Often when people complain that they can't hear the preacher, the problem is not so much with volume as articulation: sloppy speech means incomprehensible speech. Open, even exaggerated movements of jaw, lips, tongue, and teeth are necessary in the pulpit.

Having become aware of the physical apparatus of speech, we can also pay attention to how we put the words out into the air. Pitch, rate, volume, and pause are all fundamental features of oral presentation. When we read our manuscripts, we perhaps used little variation in pitch, rate, volume, or pause — it all just came out like words on the page. But now we are speaking, and can vary our pitch, rate, volume, and pause according to the needs of the content. We can provide emphasis through stress, pitch, or pause. There will be peaks and valleys as we speak. This is a primary reason to drop the manuscript and step out to preach without a net — variety is certainly the spice of oral presentation, and while we can try to write it into our manuscripts, we will never quite be able to reproduce the dynamics of conversational back-and-forth. Pitch, rate, volume, and pause allow us to *interpret* the words we are saying for the congregation. We use our voices to help people understand where we are going. We have all suffered those Scripture readings that are delivered in a deadly monotone, as if the reader had no idea what the Scripture was about. Questioned, many of those readers will tell you that they had actually been *taught* to read the Scripture that way, lest their voices add any "interpretation"! But every reading is an interpretation — the one these folks are offering is simply stained-glass and lifeless. We preachers do not want to leave our sermons uninterpreted — we, if anyone, should have an idea what we are saying! We can use our voices to help our words communicate. Ideally, we have already given some thought to pitch, rate, volume, and pause in the revision/rehearsal process, because it is part of what we have come here to say Sunday morning.

Though I have placed an emphasis on words throughout this book, preaching is not just words. Indeed, there are those who never hear a word — this is why many churches have sermons translated into sign language for the deaf. To dispense with a manuscript and preach without a net is to learn that preaching is truly a bodily function. It involves our hands, our face, our eyes. Our hearers are also viewers (except of course, for those in the congregation who are blind or hard of sight). Our entire bodies are at work in the pulpit.

Preaching without a net will allow us to cultivate an oral style that includes visuality. People will be *looking* as they listen, and we will want to give some thought to what they will see. There is no need to approach this artificially, in the manner of the famous conductor, known for his wild, theatrical gestures, who kept a close guard on his musical scores; one day a few members of the orchestra got a peek and found every scowl, every wave noted at its precise spot in the score! We preachers need not write our physical gestures into our manuscripts. A better approach is to allow the revision/rehearsal process to do its part. As we experience the sermon in rehearsal, our bodies will respond naturally. We will be internalizing not only the words but our physical responses. Gestures and facial movements will seem natural — as spontaneous as the words themselves — because they have been properly rehearsed and learned by heart. We have practiced with hands, face, and eyes as well as mouth.

This is why there must be some bodily preparation for preaching. Many homileticians recommend stretching, vocal exercises, and relaxation techniques for the preacher who is about to preach, much as for singers and actors. We will be using our entire bodies to produce the sermon; we are athletes of the soul. We prepare our bodies to integrate our words with our being. Back when we wrote a manuscript on Saturday and saved a few seconds during the sermon hymn for a second glance, we felt disconnected and alienated from the sermon — it was just words accumulated on a lectern, not something that was part of us. Our revision/rehearsal process allowed us to take the scroll and eat, to see whether it was like honey or vinegar; by Sunday it will have seeped into every part of our bodies, waiting to be let out. Some stretching, meditation, perhaps even a little singing before the service are not out of line for what will be — even if we stand unmoving in one place throughout the sermon — an athletic endeavor.

Even with proper physical preparation, some preachers experience delivery problems. A foremost concern for many congregations is the problem of volume. "We need a microphone," is a cry heard in churches throughout the land, even though in many cases, volume is not really the problem. Poor vocal production can make speech hard to hear, and amplifying it will only make the problem worse. Even if the problem is volume, amplified sound reproduction in a church is a complex matter, and I've seen instances where professionals have botched the job. Preachers had best work to develop their voices so that they can fill the room with or without a microphone — with proper breath control and resonance, they should be able to bounce their voices off the back wall. It would be well worth the money for the preacher to consult with a speech specialist to develop the voice. If amplification is available, the preacher often must project into the first few rows in order to be heard there. Microphone technique is another aspect where preachers may need training; microphones are usually directional, and will have a sweet spot that produces maximum results, and other spots that will sound thin, weak, or not at all.

Another problem preachers, especially beginners, may have is stage fright. Nervousness before or during the sermon can manifest itself in several ways: fingers fiddling, nervous tics, hands clamping on the sides of the pulpit. This nervousness should be recognized for what it is — energy — and channeled into the delivery of the sermon. A large part of stage fright is dissipated by proper preparation and experience. If you follow the steps I have laid out in this book, you will be ready to preach on Sunday, manuscript or no. There will not be anything to be frightened of. When you stand to preach, use your nervous energy to animate your delivery. Don't be afraid that your gestures will be too much — remember that stage actors make broad moves because they must be seen at a distance. If you still have extra nervous energy, try clasping your hands behind your back for a moment or two; you can clench as hard as you want, and no one will see you.

We have already mentioned some of the problems that are caused by faulty vocal production. Most of these problems are solved by relaxation, improved breath support, or greater attention to articulation. Too much nasal resonance is cured by opening the jaw wide. Stridency is cured by relaxing the neck. Mumbling is the result of lazy lips, tongue, and teeth. Hoarseness is usually a matter of breath support.

Other preacher's problems are often a matter of preparation and concentration. Word misuse and mispronunciation are a matter of continuing education; when in doubt, open the dictionary. Monotone and poor pacing are a matter of inadequate vocal interpretation of a written text, and usually cured by the revision/rehearsal process. Speech tics ("you know," "uh," "ur") are a result of nervousness, inattention, and (sometimes) inadequate preparation. Visual distractions such as fiddling with jewelry are also a matter of nervousness or inattention — if you notice you are doing something like this, stop! Sometimes it helps to call special attention to the problem; if you keep fiddling with your ring, take it off for the sermon, or tie a red ribbon around it — but you'll want to keep your hands behind your back!

Sometimes we will not be aware of our delivery problems. This is the sort of thing that people talk about behind our backs, not to our faces. After all, they don't want to hurt our feelings. And besides, they may not even know what the problem is, let alone how to correct it. It may well be that the preacher can commission some observers in the congregation to give specific feedback, informally and individually or as an organized group. If the preacher has hired a speech consultant as part of a continuing education plan, have the consultant do some work on Sunday morning; an objective, knowledgeable observer to an actual preaching event could be of great help. There is also something to be said for the use of video and audio taping for assessment and correction of preaching problems — though this may best be done with the added perspectives of a feedback group, a group of peers, or a consultant, since tapes produce a reality of their own that is different from live delivery. Also, we tend to be too hard on ourselves, when we see or hear ourselves on tape.

The problem that most frightens beginners is the prospect of memory lapse. "What if I get into the pulpit and forget something?" Again, if you have followed all the steps in this book, you are not likely to forget what you intend to say. If you take baby steps as you move toward preaching without a net, you will be able to train yourself without excessive fear of memory lapse, for there will be something to fall back on. Plus, there is the advantage of time, training, and habit; the more you practice this method of sermon presentation, the fewer and fewer your memory lapses will be. It's been years since I have had any sort of memory lapse during preaching. But this is also to make the admission that yes, you may and probably will have a memory lapse from time to time. Fortunately, a memory lapse need not mean that you fall off the tightrope, for there are several tricks you can use to get yourself moving again. The crucial rule is never to admit that you have forgotten something, and never apologize. Don't let people know that anything is amiss. There is nothing wrong with pausing to consider what comes next — if you have been in the habit of incorporating pause into your delivery when appropriate, no one will even notice that anything is wrong. If the pause does not refresh you, one trick you can use is to repeat the previous line or phrase; this is often enough to get the juices flowing again. If the repetition does not help you to remember the next line, skip ahead to a line you do remember. Yes, you may thereby skip over a line you loved — but maybe you can work it in later (remember, we are still in a process of revision, even as we preach, because the process has allowed us to develop a kind of spontaneity that we did not have when we were bound to our manuscripts). Ditto for an entire section skipped — maybe you can come

> Be prepared for memory lapses. Never let them see you sweat. Realize that most memory lapses are the fault of faulty composition.

back to it, or maybe it did not belong at all, and your subconscious mind was telling you to make this one last edit. If you get stuck and can't remember anything, ad lib until memory returns — you studied all week, so you know enough about the subject that you won't embarrass yourself. When the sermon is over (and you *will* get through it — this has been just a bump in the road), you will want to review the memory lapse for what it tells you about your preparation. Memory lapses due to inadequate rehearsal/revision, or the failure to learn the lines by heart, are solved by taking the proper time to do the work. More likely, your lapse will point out a problem in the actual composition of the sermon. I have found that most often memory lapses are caused by faults in composition, the result of structure that did not hang together, or material that was out of place, or did not belong in the sermon at all.

Occasionally beginners experience problems when they try to remember *too much* at once: they try to skip ahead to remember what's coming before they get there. In that case, just relax and let the sermon come. You have done your memory work; now is the time to trust the process.

I imagine that most preachers who are afraid to enter the paperless pulpit for the first time underestimate the power of their own memories. The brain is a resilient and capable muscle, as long as we exercise it. Those who follow the method I have proposed on a weekly basis will find that their capacity to remember their sermons will increase with regular practice. Trust your memory, trust the system. Let the sermon flow.

People simply want someone who will talk to them as one human being to another, saying something significant enough to be worth spending the time.

Many of our problems in the pulpit will dissipate once we learn to mentally and spiritually prepare for the sermon in the last few moments before we begin to preach. Now is the time for that last minute prayer, "Let the words of my mouth..." to be said in silence. Prepare physically with one last little stretch of the arm behind the back. A bit of mental adjustment may be called for:

remember why you are here, and what good news you have brought with you. Think of your congregation as being for you and not against you (however the last committee meeting may have made you feel); a little positive energy can only help the gospel. When you step up to speak, use your mouth before you open it: smile.

In the end, talk. Simply talk. That's all they want of you anyway. They simply want someone who will talk to them as one human being to another, saying something significant enough to be worth spending the time. This is what this book has been about all along — the process of simply saying what you have to say to people who want to hear it. You have good news. They want to hear it. Talk to your people. Stand and speak.

The Secret of Preaching Without a Net

Prepare like crazy, so that you are overprepared.

Structure your sermon to be memorable.

Write every word to be spoken, in as concrete and memorable language as possible.

Revise while you rehearse your sermon, with the goal of learning every word by heart.

Deliver knowing what you want to say word-by-word, but feeling free to revise right down to the last minute.

Enjoy yourself!

Sample Sermon Manuscripts

Preaching cannot be taught in the abstract, but only in the doing. It would be unfair of me to pontificate on preaching without actually doing some preaching of my own. Much as I would like to invite you to church on Sunday, here I can only give you a sample of what you might have heard, had you been there. In the spirit of "Show, don't tell," I offer these examples.

For each sermon manuscript, I've included an introduction that addresses some of the homiletical issues involved. My hope is that the sermons, with their introductions, will stand as practical illustrations of the results that can be obtained with the method I've proposed in this book.

All of these samples were preached without a net — I used no notes or manuscripts in their delivery (you will see that I have retained the original "oral manuscript" form of each sermon). They are examples of what can be done with the process outlined in this book. They were delivered pretty much as given here, though I am always editing and revising up to the moment I open my mouth. As such, they are merely written reminders of what was said — not the sermons themselves. What I cannot reproduce here are the gestures and voice that brought the words to life; the sermon was a vocal, bodily interpretation of these words. For maximum benefit and to come as close as possible to reproducing the experience, I suggest you read the manuscripts aloud.

Sermon composition is never done in isolation from the community that receives it, so a few words about specific congregations are in order. Christ Episcopal Church in Avon, Connecticut, is a medium-sized parish in a well-off suburb of Hartford; the architecture is modern, the parish young, the people prosperous. Grace and St. Peter's Church in Hamden, Connecticut, outside

New Haven, is the product of a successful merger of two diverse congregations, and while its ethos is strictly middle-class, it has accumulated a substantial endowment. I served both parishes as an Interim Ministry Specialist, and these sermons reflect the transitional dynamics at work.

Dog/God

Proper 9, Year B
Mark 6:1-6 — "Prophets are not without honor, except in their hometown."
July 9, 2000

Sometimes our sermon study uncovers a tidbit that is not common knowledge, but crucial for understanding the scriptural passage. Sometimes, as in this case, what is uncovered is just the tip of an iceberg. The ancient Mediterranean honor/shame dynamic is essential to understanding not only the reaction to Jesus' sermon in Nazareth, but much of the social dynamics reflected in the New Testament. This sermon seeks to give the congregation this clue in order to open up the text theologically. You may note that my interpretation of the Nazareth sermon in Mark is quite different from my view of Luke's version of the story, which will appear later in this book. The literary and theological diversity of the Bible can and must be reflected from the pulpit; it simply won't do to color Mark with Luke's pen. It was preached at Grace and St. Peter's Episcopal Church, Hamden, Connecticut.

I saw a bumper sticker the other day.
    It said, "My Boss is a Jewish Carpenter" —
    I thought that strange.
    Shouldn't it read, "My Boss *was* a Jewish Carpenter"?
    Jesus isn't in Nazareth anymore.

But that's the problem with bumper stickers.
    My father would never allow a bumper sticker to be put on his
        car.

147

We used to visit family in Chattanooga, Tennessee, which was Bumper Sticker Heaven: See Rock City. Visit Ruby Falls. Ride the Incline. Confederama.

My brothers and I would beg for bumper stickers.

But my father would always say, "The problem with bumper stickers is they never come off."

Just ask anyone with a twelve-year-old car that reads: Vote Dukakis.

Of course the other side would be rejoicing that what goes around comes around, if only they didn't have to scrape off the name Quayle.

The problem with bumper stickers is that they never let you change your mind.

And if Chattanooga is Bumper Sticker Heaven, then Nazareth in Jesus' day was Bumper Sticker Hell.

And now I'm not talking about the things that you paste on the back of your car, but the things you paste on the inside of your head.

Jesus walked into his hometown and began to do what he did in all the towns he visited: he began to teach in the synagogue.

But the people of Nazareth saw and heard only what they were expecting:

The carpenter.

The son of Mary.

The brother of James and Joses and Judas and Simon and all his sisters.

They could not see who he really was.

Only the carpenter.

Part of this is familiarity.

I read somewhere about a guy who went to Yellowstone to see Old Faithful.

Every twenty-four minutes the geyser erupts, and there's actually a clock that ticks down the time.

This guy was sitting next door in the Old Faithful Inn, having lunch.

Everyone in the place was watching the clock.

When it got down to one, the tourists would jump up from their tables and go to the big picture windows to watch the water show.

This guy went to the window with everyone else.

At the window, he turned around to see that all the waiters took this opportunity to sweep down on the tables and clear dishes and fill water glasses.

It was as if they all moved on cue.

Not a one of the staff looked up to watch the geyser.

They had seen it.

This is why preachers hardly ever go back to serve the congregations that sent them off for ordination.

Except, of course, for that one very painful sermon right after you get out of seminary, where you preach the prophetic word, but all they do afterwards is smile and pat you on the head and say, "I remember when you were this tall."

If they hear anything, it's only to respond, "So *that's* what they're teaching in seminaries these days."

Yet it was not just familiarity in Nazareth.

It was also *honor* and *shame.*

Ancient Palestine had a highly-developed code of honor and shame, as many societies still do today.

The most important thing that you could do was to follow the code, to act with honor. The worst thing you could do was to bring shame on your family.

This is one of the reasons, I think, that they call him "the son of Mary," and not, as would be the normal custom, "the son of Joseph."

It was the oldest son's responsibility to take care of his mother.

Joseph is presumably gone, so the honor falls to Jesus — and he's out and about, preaching in synagogues, healing the sick, casting out demons — *not* taking care of his mother.

149

It doesn't make any difference that he's got four other brothers to help out.

It was *his* job.

But there's a little more to it than that.

This was not a pull-yourself-up-by-your-sandalstraps kind of place.

You were a carpenter; that is what you were trained to do; that is what you were *born* to do.

You didn't get above yourself.

Educated people, rich people with time on their hands and clean fingernails, studied the Torah and taught in the synagogue.

Not the carpenter.

The carpenter certainly did *not* leave town and go to other towns preaching the Kingdom of God and yada yada yada yada.

They were offended at him — deeply, mortally offended.

In their way of looking at it, Jesus had brought shame.

Even his own family thought he was crazy, Mark tells us.

So Jesus said, "Prophets are not without *honor*, except in their hometown, and among their own kin, and in their own house."

And yet there's even more going on here than shame and honor.

There's also the monkey factor.

In India, the time-honored method for catching monkeys is to use a coconut shell.

You take half of the shell and put a hole in it just large enough for a monkey to squeeze a hand through.

Then you pin the shell to the ground, and put some food inside of it.

The monkey will come along, smell the food, and wiggle his hand down inside to grab the food.

But then the monkey is trapped, because no monkey is ever going to drop a bit of food, and there's no way to get its hand out of the hole, as long as it's closed in a fist.

All the hunter has to do is come along and collect the monkey.

The people of Nazareth, along with the rest of the human race, share the monkey factor.

There's no way we're going to let go, once we get something in our fists.

You live in Nazareth, you know that Messiahs come from heaven in power and glory. They do not apprentice as carpenters.

Crucified people do not become the Son of God, nor do bands of ex-fishermen constitute the people of God.

Bread and wine do not become body and blood, any more than a couple of dozen people sitting in a white building in Hamden, Connecticut, could be God's hope for this world.

We get it in our fists, there's no way we'll let it go.

Mark tells us that Jesus could do little or nothing in Nazareth.

His power was limited by their disbelief.

But then Mark tells us the most important part of the story:

Mark says simply, "He went about among the other villages teaching."

Because if people are like monkeys, then God is like a dog.

In particular, God is like the most famous dog in Japan, Hatchiko.

Americans have Lassie; the Japanese have Hatchiko.

Hatchiko used to go with her master to the train station every day to see him off to work.

And every evening at 5:00 p.m. Hatchiko would return to the train station to wait for her master to come home.

One day the master did not come home. He had died that day at work.

Hatchiko waited for him at the station at 5:00 o'clock, as always.

In fact, so the story goes, Hatchiko the dog came to the station every day at 5:00 o'clock, for the next eleven years, for the rest of her life.

Jesus kept going; he kept on teaching.

Even though we human beings keep holding on to that which is not worth our lives.

God keeps coming back, keeps waiting, doggedly waiting for us.

Accident Report

Proper 10, Year C
Luke 10:25-37 — "Who is my neighbor?"
July 12, 1998

This sermon, which was preached at Christ Episcopal Church in Avon, Connecticut, is set along a main road that leads from Avon toward Hartford (the insurance capital of the world). It is an example of a sermon that takes its form from the Scripture in a very direct fashion — it simply retells the Scripture in modern guise (and to be honest, owes no little inspiration to Clarence Jordan's *Cotton Patch Gospel*). The problem with this particular parable of Jesus is that its message has been obscured by layers of sentimentality; we no longer think of the main character as scum (as Jesus' contemporaries did), but as a hero. The thing I pondered was how to recapture that sense of shock and disbelief that the original parable must have invoked among its hearers, and yet still move my congregation in a positive direction. The reader can judge how well I've done here; I can certainly report that some people in Avon were shocked. Others in this media-saturated, positivistic culture were merely surprised that I could "know" about these events — had I seen it on television? I wonder if Jesus had the same problem.

A man was carjacked the other day on Route 4 outside Farmington.
> He didn't see it coming.
> It was early, not even 6:00 a.m.; he was hoping to get an early start on his workday down at Aetna.
> He was sitting at the intersection, waiting for the light, listening to a CD, thinking about the day's To-Do list.
> He hadn't even thought to press the door lock button on his Lexus.

One of them came through the passenger side with a gun.

The other pulled him out the driver's side like he was nothing more than a sack of potatoes.

They pistol-whipped him, knocked the wind out of him, and smacked him a couple of extra times for resisting.

They tore his suit.

They took his wallet and his watch and even his Italian loafers.

They kicked him in the head one last time before they drove off in his car.

Of course by that time he had already passed out.

The first car that came along was driven by an Episcopal priest.

He was on his way to officiate at an early service at the Cathedral.

Afterwards he had a very important meeting with the Bishop that morning. They were planning an addition to the parish hall at his church, and a big celebration for the hundredth anniversary of the congregation. Things were going well, booming.

He saw the man with the torn suit and no shoes on the side of the road.

At first he didn't think much of it — about what he expected to see when driving into the city, just another one sleeping it off.

But he wasn't in the city yet, and when he passed by he could see that the man was hurt.

He thought about stopping, but then he'd be late for the service. And it's awfully hard to get an appointment with the Bishop, and there was that deadline for the loan application for the addition.

He prayed a little prayer as he punched 911 on his cell phone.

911 put him on hold.

After a few minutes, he passed out of range, and the phone disconnected.

The next car that passed by held three people who all worked with the man at Aetna.

They were on their way to an early morning ecumenical prayer breakfast downtown.

One was on the planning committee of the prayer breakfast and was scheduled to deliver the opening prayer.

The other two were members of the board at their own churches.

They saw the man in the torn suit and no shoes on the side of the road.

They didn't recognize him.

One of them said, "Looks like the guy's hurt."

Another said, "You know, sometimes gangs will set out a decoy, someone to play dead, and when you stop to help they jump you."

The driver kept driving.

One of them dialed 911 on a cell phone.

Another said, "Nice suit."

911 put them on hold, the car passed out of range, and the phone disconnected.

The third car that passed thumped with rap music.

The driver wore a leather jacket, wrap-around shades, and rings in his nose and eyelids.

He was a drug dealer.

He saw the man on the side of the road, and he knew a mugging when he saw it.

He pulled over and got out to take a look.

It was obvious the guy was in pretty bad shape.

The drug dealer patted him down — no wallet, no watch, no nothing, but he did have a pulse.

So the drug dealer pulled the man over his shoulder, dragged him to his car, and put him in the backseat.

He drove to the emergency room of the hospital.

He stopped in front of the door and went around to the back to pull the man out.

A security guard called across the parking lot to him, "You can't park there. Ambulances only."

The drug dealer ignored him. He took the man inside and laid him on the closest empty gurney, and wheeled him through the double doors.

A nurse took over, wheeled the man into an alcove, and began to work on him.

The drug dealer turned to go.

Somebody with a nametag stopped him: "Wait a minute. We need proof of insurance."

"Oh, man's got insurance all right," said the drug dealer.

"We need proof of payment."

The drug dealer pulled a roll of cash out of his pocket, and peeled off a couple of hundred dollar bills. "This do?"

Behind him the security guard said, "You'll have to move your car."

That night, the Episcopal priest met with the Vestry to plan the new addition.

The three insurance executives all had dinner at home with their families.

And the drug dealer took up his post, watching the white kids who drove in from the suburbs as soon as the sun went down.

The man who had been mugged woke up that night in the hospital confused and disoriented.

"Don't try to sit up," the nurse said. "You've had a concussion. Can you tell me your name and address? Your family must be worried by now."

"How did I get here?" he said.

"I don't know," the nurse said. "Someone found you and brought you in. Must have been one of your neighbors."

The man said, "Who is my neighbor?"

The Gospel According To Bart

Epiphany 4, Year B
Deuteronomy 18:15-20 — "The Lord will raise up for you from
among you a prophet like me." and Mark 1:21-28 — "What is
this? A new teaching — with authority!"
January 30, 2000

I am sometimes accused of using pop culture in my preaching. I don't feel the need to apologize. Quite the opposite. To say that my preaching style is influenced by the culture of the day is nothing to me but a compliment. Gradations in culture are largely a matter of taste, and as we all know, the taste of our congregations varies widely. After this sermon, there were people who were happy to tell me that they had never watched Bart Simpson (fortunately I told the story in the way they could follow, even without being familiar with the characters), but there were just as many people in the congregation who had never read a lick of Graham Greene, or would never go to see a movie like *The End of the Affair,* which I cite at the end of this sermon. It seems to me that preaching has to reach both audiences. Show, don't tell, must for this reason be our rule, no matter what the content. We can't assume they know Bart or Barth; whatever we glean from our study, we must show it to them so they can appreciate it on its own and for itself. This sermon was preached at Grace and St. Peter's Episcopal Church, Hamden, Connecticut.

Bart Simpson is out of time.

It is the night before the big test, and he needs to pass, not only to avoid flunking the course, but to move on to the next grade.

One more "F," and he will be held back to repeat the whole year.

It is lights out, bedtime, and he is not ready for the test.

So he does what a lot of people do when times get desperate: He prays.

"Dear God," Bart says, "you held back the sun for Moses. Give me one more day to study."

"Prayer, the last refuge of the scoundrel," says his sister Lisa.

But the next day a freak snowstorm sweeps in and covers Springfield, giving Bart one more day.

"I'm no theologian," says Lisa later, totally flabbergasted. "All I know is that the Lord is a force more powerful than Mom and Dad put together, and you owe God big."

"Yes," says Bart, clutching his test, "part of this D-minus belongs to God."

If speaking to God is serious business, speaking for God is something else entirely.

I read in the newspaper that the New York State welfare office will no longer refer its clients to jobs at the Psychic Friends Network.

No longer can you call 1-800-PSYCHIC and pay four dollars ninety-nine cents a minute to speak directly to a New York welfare mother.

It's too bad for the welfare mothers, because apparently it was nice work — the pay was good, and all you needed to apply was a pleasant, sympathetic telephone voice.

And, oh, yes, what if you weren't actually psychic? That's okay, said the Psychic Friends. We train.

It reminds me of the psychic hotline that went out of business a few years ago, because, a spokesperson said, they had financial difficulties they could not foresee.

The people of Israel were told right off not to waste their $4.99.

"When you come into the land the Lord your God is giving you," said Moses, "do not do what the people of the land do — "

158

Keep away from soothsayers, sorcerers, witches, mediums, necromancers, psychics trained or untrained.

If you have something to say to God, you can get down on your knees and say it directly.

And if you want to hear something from God, you will have from God a prophet.

"The Lord your God will raise up for you from among you a prophet like me," Moses told them.

Moses said a couple of important things about this prophet.

One is that the prophet comes from "among you"; the prophet is one of your brothers and sisters, a fellow Israelite.

You don't have to consult anyone from the outside, Moses said. It will be one of you.

One of our friends just started working on the staff of an Episcopal Diocese in New England.

The bishop introduced her to the convention, and rattled off all of her experience and her qualifications for the job.

Last of all, and "Best of all," said the bishop, "she is a native New Englander."

And they all started cheering.

There's something about being "one of us" that gains you the credibility to do the job.

The prophet will be one of you.

The other thing about that prophet, said Moses, is that the prophet will be like me.

That's not just his big head talking.

It's fundamental to the whole plot.

The prophet is going to look like something familiar, Moses said.

The prophet is going to hold you accountable to what you already know.

You have to remember that by the time we get to the book of Deuteronomy, we're at the fifth of five books of Moses.

We're talking about all the traditions that have been gathered around the name of Moses — not just whatever Moses actually wrote, and we know he didn't write all of it himself —

But all the accumulated wisdom that extends back through the line of Moses.

That's five thick detailed books —

This is what the prophet is going to have to look like, said Moses.

It's not so much like being psychic or telling the future; the Old Testament prophet looks backward as much as forward, or rather the prophet looks at the present in light of the past.

The prophet is someone with moral courage, who can look at society with an eye trained by Moses, and say, this, and not that, is how things should be.

The prophet stands up in a corrupt court, next to the unbalanced scales of justice, and points back to the ideal.

There's really nothing new about this prophet.

It's all in the library.

It's a lot of bedtime reading.

You try reading the first five books of the Bible at two or three chapters a night, and see how long it takes you to get through it all.

Genesis alone will take you almost a month at that rate.

And that's without all the commentary.

By the time we move from Deuteronomy to the days of Jesus, there's another half-a-millennium of tradition to deal with.

It's no wonder that the people of Israel could not come to a consensus about this new prophet in their midst.

There was so much material to wade through.

A good deal of the New Testament was written to prove that Jesus was in fact the prophet like Moses.

We get an early glimpse into the issue in Mark's story about what happened at the synagogue in Capernaum.

160

Any Jewish man could be invited to teach in the synagogue, so it was no particular surprise when Jesus stood up to speak.

Even what he had to say wasn't particularly new — the prophet like Moses will sound something like Moses.

It was the way Jesus said things —

"Not as the scribes," Mark tells us, "but as one who had authority."

Apparently what they were used to was commentary on the commentary, an endless parade of quotes and citations and "So-and-so says this but Thus-and-thus says that."

Somebody was telling me the story the other day, about the Sunday school class that was learning proper church behavior.

"Why is it important to be quiet during the sermon?" asked the teacher.

"Because," said one little girl, "people are sleeping."

Maybe the expectation in the synagogue was no greater.

But no eyelids grew heavy as Jesus taught.

Just as no one could sleep through the cries of the unclean spirit that interrupted the sermon.

"What have you to do with us, Jesus of Nazareth? Have you come to destroy us, you Holy One of God?"

"Shut up," said Jesus, "and come out!"

After Jesus finished off the demon, they were even more amazed.

Moses had power to do signs and wonders in the courts of Pharaoh, and here was Jesus with authority even over the unseen powers of evil.

"What is this?" they said to one another. "A new teaching — with authority!"

They were flabbergasted.

But, you know, "amazed" is not the same as "believed."

In fact, Mark usually uses that word "amazed" to describe the people who don't believe in Jesus.

161

He tells us that Jesus' *fame* spread through the countryside, but he does not say that the whole countryside came to *faith*.

Because it's one thing to see the prophet like Moses, and another to recognize him.

With recognition comes responsibility.

You have to realize that you are accountable for what you see and hear.

If it's truly God speaking, you're not going to be able just to hang up that phone.

You're going to owe big.

There's a movie out now, *The End of the Affair*, starring Julianne Moore as a woman named Sarah living in London in the middle of the Blitz, in World War II.

Without giving too much of the movie away, I can tell you that the pivotal scene finds Sarah on her knees by the side of her bed in the rubble, praying her heart out for the one thing that means more to her than life itself.

As we watch, her prayer comes true.

Her life from that moment undergoes electric shock treatment. She cannot go on as before. She will never be the same again.

You cannot let God into the deepest part of your heart without coming away scorched.

Later on Sarah will say that as much as she tried to resist it, "On that day, a love was born."

Now theologically, I would say that Sarah's prayer was no more mature than Bart Simpson's.

Prayer is more than getting what you asked for.

Just as a prophet does more than tell your future.

And listening to the word is more than staying awake through the sermon.

But Sarah's prayer was a start.

All God needs is a little crack to slip through.

Faith is a little seed, and worship and teaching are the sun and
the rain that make faith grow.
The real test of faith is what happens next.

The Power Of The Python

Easter 7, Year C
Acts16:16-34 — "These men are slaves of God, who proclaim to you a way of salvation."
May 27, 2001

I include this sermon because it presents a problem of memory, and because the problem was solved. The Seuss-like rhyme of the opening (no one seems to know where this poem came from, Dr. Seuss didn't remember writing it, and it exists on the Internet in enough variations to make a textual critic drool) was the hardest part to learn by heart, since I did not write it. It had the advantage of rhythm and rhyme, but the memory work was still much harder than with my usual sermons. The solution was simply to spend more time with it. Most of our memory problems are fixed either by revision, if the problem is structural, or as in this case, by more rehearsal. Was it worth it? (I could have started the sermon with "You have to make a choice"). Yes, if for no other reason, delight — not the least of which was the delight I saw on their faces as they gradually realized that my opening lines were not ordinary. One of the joys of preaching at Grace and St. Peter's Episcopal Church was the creativity of the congregation — there were a number of Suess lovers who after the service gave me their own Suessian evaluation of the sermon, complete with rhymes. Here's a footnote: the final story came from Desiree Cooper and was aired on *All Things Considered,* May 24, 2001.

Did I ever tell you about the young Zoad
Who came to two signs at a fork in the road?
One said, "place one" and the other, "place two."
So the Zoad had to make up his mind what to do.

164

Well the Zoad scratched his head, his chin, and his pants,
And he said to himself, "Now, I'll be taking a chance.
"If I go to place one, that place may be hot.
"So how will I know if I like it or not?
"On the other hand though, I'll feel such a fool,
"If I go to place two and find it's too cool.
"In that case I may catch a chill and turn blue.
"So place one may be best and not place two.
"On the other hand though, if place one is too high,
"I might get a terrible earache and die.
"On the other hand though, if place two is too low,
"I might get some terrible pain in my toe.
"So place one may be the best," and he started to go.
And he stopped and he said, "On the other hand though ...
"On the other hand, other hand, other hand though ..."
And for thirty-six hours and one half that Zoad
Made starts and made stops at the fork in the road,
Saying, "No, don't take a chance; you may not be right."
Then he got an idea that was wonderfully bright.
"Play safe!" cried the Zoad. "I'll play safe. I'm no dunce.
"I'll simply start off to both places at once."
And that's how the Zoad who would not take a chance
Got to no place at all with a split in his pants.
    — Anonymous, sometimes attributed to Dr. Seuss

You have to make a choice.

    That was what was so annoying to Paul.

    It was not just the persistent drip, drip, drip —

    Day after day of the slave girl and her singsong voice:

    "These men are slaves of the Most High God, who proclaim
        to you a way of salvation."

    What annoyed Paul so much was the fact that she spoke the
        truth —

    Yet she was unable to live that truth.

    She was under the power of the Python.

Our translation calls it "a spirit of divination," but any citizen in the Roman colony of Philippi would have recognized the Python —

That great mythical dragon who rose out of the mud to rule Delphi.

The snake was slain by Apollo, but was still said to inspire the priestesses of the Delphic Oracle, where people would come to ask questions about their future, and get a thumbs up or thumbs down on their plans.

The Romans thought that all fortune-telling came from spirits like the Python, so even this little slave girl could be a priestess of the snake.

She had the spirit of the serpent.   .

Paul, of course, had a different view of the snake —

The pages of Genesis and Revelation and all that lies in-between see the Python in a less-positive light.

The snake is something to be avoided —

The dragon a force to be fought.

As far as Paul was concerned, this little girl was under the bondage of the devil, and she must be freed.

The Book of Acts treats the story like an exorcism, just like Jesus —

Paul commanded the spirit of the Python to exit:

"I order you in the name of Jesus Christ to come out of her."

And it came out that very hour.

Which is when we find what this was really about.

It was about money.

This was a traveling freak show.

Gypsies with corporate sponsors.

What really counted was ticket sales.

The owners of the slave girl were making a living off the fortune-seekers.

People then and now would pay good money to the Psychic Friends Network.

166

And as Paul found out, you don't want to make the Psychic
Friends your enemies.
With the spirit of the Python gone, there would be no more
fortune-telling.
And someone was going to have to pay.

Paul and Silas, being the most suitable someones, were dragged
off to the authorities.
Lies were told, half truths.
You never went wrong playing to the fears of the Roman
public.
You can say anything, as long as you know the buttons to push:
Blame it on the Jews, blame it on foreigners.
You know, those people just aren't like us.

Nowadays, Paul and Silas would have simply been subjected to a
lashing on talk radio.
But this was a more brutally honest place and time.
They took the concept of deterrent seriously, and what could
not be seen was not going to deter.
Punishment was public as well as bloody.
It was the ultimate reality show, and you did not have to wait
until prime time:
"Real Life Danger in the Public Square": "Evangelists on Trial:
You Make the Call" —
Dial 1-900-THUMBSUP or THUMBSDOWN.
Most people in that marketplace that day were holding their
thumbs down.
Paul and Silas were stripped and lashed and beaten with rods.
Thirty-nine lashes were the customary punishment, for it was
said that on the fortieth lash, you would certainly die.
Only then was it off to jail, maximum security, with feet in the
stocks.

And that's where we find them, singing.
Singing!

What kind of person do you have to be, to be singing at a time
  like this?
What kind of spirit has gotten into you?
Most people I know find their very belief in God tried by the
  slightest setback in life.
I personally would be happier at home in the La-Z-Boy.
But here were Paul and Silas, the blood still oozing from the
  welts in their backs, their feet up not in recliners but in
  chains, and they "were praying and singing hymns to God,
  and the prisoners were listening to them."
Not only had they kept their faith through the torture, but they
  continued to proclaim it.

Which was when they got a big assist from on high.
Jesus promised release to the captives, and Paul and Silas got
  to take that promise quite literally —
As did everyone else in that jail that night, as the foundation
  shook and the doors swung open and the chains unlinked.
Even the jailer was saved by Paul that night, as his sword of
  honor was stopped in midair by Paul's words: "Do not
  harm yourself, your prisoners are all still here" —
Those words, and the other words Paul used in answer to the
  question, "What must I do to be saved?"
"Believe in the Lord Jesus Christ, and you will be saved, and
  all your household."

After all this, I think it's safe to say that we should be on high
  symbolism alert as we finish the story —
We watch the jailer take Paul and Silas into his own house.
He washed their wounds.
He and his whole now-baptized family invited their new broth-
  ers to the table.
I don't think it's any accident that these people who were just
  baptized immediately begin to serve wounded humanity
  and gather together for a meal.
What else would you do, once you've been "saved"?

There was a story on the radio the other day about a black woman named Desi who moved into what had once been an all-white neighborhood.

Rumor had it that Joe and Bev, the white people next door, were racists.

Joe and Bev had been hostile when black people had moved into the neighborhood thirty years earlier.

The story had it that when one of the new black neighbors had come over to introduce himself, Joe had looked at the dark extended hand and refused to touch it.

So Desi kept her distance. A friendly wave as you pass by, a nod of the head, but nothing more — no harm in being nice, why put your feelings on the line for people who will just hurt you?

But as time went by, the boundaries between the two houses loosened; the kids would go over into Bev and Joe's yard to retrieve a football or a frisbee, and come back with a ginger snap or a quarter.

And after Joe died, Bev would be on the phone, wanting one of the kids to help her carry groceries or lift a potted plant, and they would come back with vegetables from Bev's garden, or a box of popsicles.

Was Bev just being friendly now because she was lonely? Did she think of these children as her servants?

One day Desi came home to find a message from Bev: "Hi, Desi, I need your opinion on something — you're just like a daughter to me."

And there was Bev at her front door, in a dusky rose dress and string of pearls.

"I'm going out of town," she said as she hustled into the living room, "and I wanted to know if this looked okay. I've just had it altered, and look what they did with the lining."

The next thing Desi knew, Bev had whipped off the dress.

And Desi found herself wondering how it came to be that she was standing there with this person she had made it a point to keep away from, and now this person was half-naked in her living room, the two of them like mother

169

and daughter, a couple of girlfriends sharing a secret, like kids at a slumber party.

When all is said and done, this is how you know it took:
God doesn't just save people; God changes people.
To be baptized is the beginning.
To believe is to be changed.

Fingerprints

Epiphany 4, Year C
Jeremiah 1:4-10 — "The Lord put out a hand and touched my
lip." and Luke 4:21-32 — "Today this scripture has been
fulfilled in your hearing."
January 28, 2001

There are some who contend that in order to preach without a net, the sermon must rely on story, and be extremely short. Unless you're telling one long story, or a series of little stories, so the theory goes, you are going to be dependent on your notes and manuscripts. And if you try to preach longer than eight to ten minutes (the average length between television commercials), you will surely lose it. Here is a counterexample; this sermon was my average length, almost fifteen minutes long, and it really has no stories at all, though it comments on two biblical stories. I did not have any problem preaching it without a manuscript of notes. This is not because I have an exceptional memory, either — though I do have a practiced one. It has more to do with the nature of the sermon itself, which was conceived from the beginning with delivery — and therefore memory — in mind. The style is story-like, in that it makes maximum use of concrete nouns and vivid verbs, in an attempt to make the sermon something that can be seen, tasted, smelled, and touched as well as heard. It is the use of language, not story form per se, that makes a sermon memorable. This sermon was preached at Grace and St. Peter's Episcopal Church, Hamden, Connecticut.

As usual, God has it backwards.
Everyone knows what this means:
The finger to the lip.
It means: Be quiet.

171

Don't speak.
Shut up.
Everyone knows that.

Except, of course, God.
"The Lord put out a hand and touched my lip," said the prophet Jeremiah.
And did God say, "Sssh"?
No.
The opposite.
"I have put my words in your mouth," the Lord told Jeremiah.
"Today I appoint you over nations and over kingdoms, to pluck up and to pull down, to destroy and to overthrow, to build and to plant."

This is the kind of thing that can ruin your whole day.
Isaiah said that when he met up with God, an angel of the Lord took a hot coal from the altar with a pair of tongs, and touched it to his lips.
How much more searing must have been the direct touch of the finger of God on the lips of Jeremiah.
Ouch!
That's got to leave a scar.
What is it like, I wonder, to walk around the rest of your life with that thing right there where everyone can see — the fingerprint of God on your lips?

If they don't seem to notice the mouth, they can hardly ignore the words.
Some people think that preachers should keep out of politics.
"It's dirty," they say. "It will soil you."
They point their fingers at the pulpit and say, "You must stop saying such things."
God, however, must have missed that memo.
Once again, the Lord has it backwards.

"I appoint you *over* nations and kingdoms," God told Jeremiah
— pluck up, pull down, destroy, overthrow, build, and
plant.
Evidently God did have something to say to the nations.
And the only way to say it was through the disfigured lips of a
prophet.
This sort of preaching is not just a rehash of what you heard
on *Nightline*:
Pundits glazed over with a bit of Scripture and a smidgen of
piety.
This is something new.
Because it does not come from any mere human being.
"You shall go where *I* send you," said the Lord to Jeremiah.
"You shall speak what *I* command."
"*I* am with you," said the Lord.

And sure enough, when the time came, Jeremiah was right there
on the op-ed page of the *Jerusalem Post*, saying the exact opposite of what everyone else had to say.
All the other prophets — the people who claimed to be prophets — told the people that no way would the Babylonians
ever take us, the People of God, from our land.
Jeremiah alone told the truth, that they would have to learn to
sing God's song by the rivers of Babylon.
The people of Jerusalem would be taken out of their city, and
they would spend seventy long years in exile.
Because it wasn't good enough just to sit back and let things
be the way they were.
Life is always changing, and God keeps asking us for that
response to the change that we call faith.
What the people needed to hear was not the regurgitation of
what they already believed.
They needed something from outside of themselves.
They needed a word from God.

The problem being that God keeps getting it backwards.
Ask anyone from the synagogue at Nazareth.
There they were, waiting for the preacher to take the pulpit.
It's the new guy.
Well, not *new* new.
You remember him.
Son of the carpenter.
I hear he's been doing great stuff all over Galilee.
I can't wait to hear what he's going to tell *us*:
His old friends.
The people he grew up with.
We're practically family.
Why, I remember him when he was *so* tall.
Just think, finally a prophet of our own in Nazareth.
On the map at last, a city on the move.
Mr. Mayor, what do you think?
It'll be like having a gold mine in our own backyard.

But no prophet is accepted by the hometown crowd.
As Luke tells the story, when Jesus got up to preach, it was no boost to the local economy.
It was not even a comfort.
Any more than Elijah was a comfort to Israel, when the heavens were shut up for three and a half years, and where did the prophet go? To a foreigner, a widow of Zarephath up north in Sidon.
No more did Elisha play to the hometown crowd, bypassing all the lepers of Israel to heal outside the walls, Naaman the Syrian.
Far from playing the local connection, Jesus all but insulted them in Nazareth.
It's not just that he refused to join the local Jaycees.
He touched a tender spot in the national psyche.
Up and down the land of Israel in Jesus' day there was that sense of privilege, the pride of being chosen God's people.
There was that feeling of being exclusive.

174

Yet their own tradition said there was more to being a Jew
than simply birthright.
And their own most famous prophets reached beyond the walls.
You can't rely on heritage, Jesus seemed to say.
God doesn't care where you came from, or what's on your
resume.
The only thing God is interested in is what you are doing now.

And it doesn't do any good to heckle the preacher.
"Hey, Jesus, we heard what you did at Capernaum; cut the
politics and do something for us."
You can't tell a prophet to shut up.
Not even under threat of being run out of town and off a cliff.
Because the prophet, the true prophet of God, has the distinc-
tive swirl of a hot fingertip on the lip.
And even after all these years, that scar still burns.

Lord, "Deliver us from the presumption of coming to this Table
for solace only, and not for strength; for pardon only, and not
for renewal." (*Book of Common Prayer*, p. 372)
I suppose there are some people who would not hesitate to get
into their little window on *Nightline* and say, "Yes, Ted,
this is the Promised Land."
But given God's penchant for getting things backwards, I would
want to be careful about that sort of thing.
If I read Jeremiah's op-ed page right, the conventional wisdom won't cut it.
And if I hear Jesus' sermon in the synagogue in Nazareth cor-
rectly, historical and cultural boundaries do not contain
God.
I suppose that there are some people who think that their baptism and profession of the Christian faith is some sort of
entitlement.
Entitlement to what, I don't know; I suppose there would be
different versions of what that baptism and faith might
entitle you to —
A spot in heaven, perhaps —

Solace in adversity —
Admission to the club — I don't know.
Maybe just the chance to sit in the pew and listen to sermons
like this one.

But I would suggest that if you think about it, baptism is actually
membership in the ranks of the prophets.
It's all in the *Book of Common Prayer*.
Think of the words that you have to say as part of the baptis-
mal covenant (pp. 303-04):
"Will you proclaim by word and example the Good News of
God in Christ?"
Sounds like prophecy to me — not telling the future, but proph-
ecy in the proper sense, speaking that word that comes
from outside of ourselves.
"Will you seek and serve Christ in all persons, loving your
neighbor as yourself?"
"Will you strive for justice and peace among all people, and
respect the dignity of every human being?"
Sounds like a prophetic message to me — maybe even a po-
litical prophetic message.
At any rate, these are words to burn the mouth.
How could we possibly say, "Yes," to those questions unless
we had at least a trace of God's finger on our lips?
Oh, maybe it would take Sherlock Holmes and his magnify-
ing glass to see it on some of us, but it's got to be there.
How else but the finger of God could anyone possibly say,
"Yes, I will, with God's help"?

Someone once asked the question: If being a Christian were ille-
gal, would there be enough evidence to convict you?
I believe that the case will be solved through good old-fashioned detective work.
The question will be answered when they test our lips for
fingerprints.

Appendix: Hints And Tips

1. The great communicators are those who manage both form and content well; they have something worthwhile to say, and they say it well.

2. The key to preaching that is both thoughtful and interesting is delivery. Delivery determines the sermon.

3. The most basic decision every preacher must make is whether to allow the nature of the sermon as an oral, communal event to have its full impact on the entire process of sermon production and delivery.

4. Cicero taught the five acts of rhetoric: *Invention, Arrangement, Style, Memory, Delivery*.

5. The Roman rhetorical tradition was designed to teach speakers to do exactly the kind of thing we want to do: speak clearly, beautifully, and apparently off-the-cuff.

6. Augustine baptized Cicero, immersing rhetorical tradition in biblical tradition.

7. Amplification and transmission have brought about a more conversational style of rhetoric.

8. Modern preaching has placed too much emphasis on writing and neglected the role of memory.

9. What cannot be remembered should not be delivered. Begin, continue, and end with memory in mind.

10. Allow one hour of preparation, including study, rehearsal, and revision, for every minute you plan to speak.

11. Our audience determines what we say and how we say it. We wish to proclaim good news, so our study begins with the lives of those who would hear that news.

12. In observing life, keep an eye out for that which is memorable.

13. Develop some means of storage and retrieval of material taken from your study of Life: a file, a box, whatever works for you.

14. Scripture is always read in community. Embrace your community and your tradition.

15. Scripture study includes ongoing continuing education for background purposes as well as the study of this week's readings.

16. Buy reference books carefully, beginning with the basics. Choose a good commentary over a prefab sermon resource booklet.

17. Spread your Scripture study out over the week, beginning with the weightiest references and moving progressively through easier material as you head towards the end of the week.

18. The weekly study of Scripture is largely a matter of keeping files, so that we can use them again for another sermon later.

19. For each Scripture reading, pay attention to context, source, form, and text, as well as the actual content.

20. Summarize your study of each passage with two sentences, dealing with content and form. Answer these questions: What does the text say? What does the text do?

21. The move from study to composition is simply a change in audience. Prepare to compose the sermon by imagining your congregation as the new audience of your study.

22. You compose a sermon; you do not write it. The sermon is nothing more or less than the words that are delivered to the congregation.

23. Sermon structures help create anticipation and unity; they are also memory aids.

24. The preacher has three choices for structure: taking forms from the text of Scripture, using a prefab form, or inventing one's own.

25. Great lines are memorable not so much for what they say as how they say it — in other words, for their style.

26. Attention to style will lend to our sermons two essential qualities: recognition and identification. It will also make our sermons more memorable.

27. Write in oral style, words not to be seen, but heard. In oral style, the author, not the listener, controls time.

28. Oral writing cuts to the bone. Short words, short sentences. Easier to listen to, easier to remember.

29. Incorporate speaking into composition from the beginning. Anticipate how it will sound.

30. Make maximum use of vivid verbs and concrete nouns. The words that are most memorable — and thus the easiest to speak and hear — are words that can evoke the senses, words that you can see, touch, taste, smell.

31. Show, don't tell. Talk about real people.

179

32. Our goal is to speak. What we write must serve our speaking. Use an oral manuscript form.

33. Nothing can be delivered that is not remembered. If you can't remember it, you probably need to revise it.

34. Final delivery is an extension of the revision/rehearsal process. The sermon is never done until it is preached, and even as it is preached, it is in the final stages of composition.

35. It is a short step from the continual re-experiencing of the sermon to the complete internalization of the words. Learning the sermon by heart is the last step of revision/rehearsal.

36. Learn the sermon by heart line-by-line, one thought-unit at a time, from the back to the front.

37. Take baby steps as you learn to preach without a net. Gradually work yourself up to using no paper at all on Sunday mornings.

38. Use the freedom of preaching without paper to improve your composition and delivery.

39. Be prepared for memory lapses. Never let them see you sweat. Realize that most memory lapses are the fault of faulty composition.

40. People simply want someone who will talk to them as one human being to another, saying something significant enough to be worth spending the time.

Bibliographic Note

Having dispensed with footnotes for readability's sake, I would like to take a few moments to acknowledge my debt to those who came before me, and to point the reader towards books worthy of further study.

My own approach to how to think about preaching, in particular how to move from the biblical text to the sermon, is found in William H. Shepherd, *No Deed Greater Than a Word: A New Approach to Biblical Preaching* (Lima, Ohio: CSS Publishing Co., 1998). Homileticians will note my obvious debt to Fred Craddock; *Overhearing the Gospel* (Beecher Lectures, 1978. Nashville: Abingdon Press, 1978) and *As One Without Authority* (Third edition. Nashville: Abingdon Press, 1979), both now in convenient reprints from Chalice Press, are still worth reading, but his most balanced work is found in *Preaching* (Nashville: Abingdon Press, 1985). Craddock in turn was indebted to the prescient classic by R. E. C. Browne, *The Ministry of the Word* (London: SCM Press, 1958), now out-of-print and hopelessly outdated in language and ethos, but still worth reading by those who can appreciate the poetry.

Cicero's works are available in many editions, and the Greco-Roman rhetorical tradition is neatly summarized in James J. Murphy, ed., *A Synoptic History of Classical Rhetoric* (Davis, CA: Hermagoras Press, 1983). Augustine's *De Doctrina Christiania* is readily available in translation (I have cited D. W. Robertson, Jr., New York: Prentice Hall, 1958), and in a critical edition by Sister Thérèse Sullivan (Instrumenta Lexicologica Latina. Turnhout: Brepols, 1982). An account of the preaching of Augustine and other patristic writers can be found in Thomas K. Carroll, *Preaching the Word* (Message of the Fathers of the Church, 11. Wilmington:

Michael Glazier, Inc., 1984). A wider view of the history of preaching is Paul Scott Wilson, *A Concise History of Preaching* (Nashville: Abingdon Press, 1992). Excerpts from great homileticians from all ages can be found in Richard Lischer, editor, *Theories of Preaching: Selected Readings in the Homiletical Tradition* (Durham: Labyrinth Press, 1987), revised as *The Company of Preachers: Wisdom on Preaching, Augustine to the Present* (Grand Rapids: Eerdmans, 2002).

The issue of the congregation's input into the sermon — and thus the reason we begin studying Life before we study Scripture each week — is discussed in my own book, *No Deed Greater Than a Word,* as well as John S. McClure, *The Roundtable Pulpit: Where Leadership and Preaching Meet* (Nashville: Abingdon, 1995), Lucy Atkinson Rose, *Sharing the Word: Preaching in the Roundtable Church* (Louisville: Westminster John Knox Press, 1997), and Lenora Tubbs Tisdale, *Preaching as Local Theology and Folk Art* (Minneapolis: Fortress Press, 1997). Keeping both preacher and congregation interested in the sermon is the subject of Robert C. Dykstra, *Discovering a Sermon: Personal Pastoral Preaching* (St. Louis: Chalice Press, 2001). The influence of the community on the sermon — and the multicultural nature of the modern Church — is addressed in Justo L. González and Catherine Gunsalus González, *Liberation Preaching: The Pulpit and the Oppressed* (Abingdon Preacher's Library. Nashville: Abingdon, 1980), Henry H. Mitchell, *Black Preaching: The Recovery of a Powerful Art* (Nashville: Abingdon Press, 1990), and Thomas H. Troeger, *The Parable of Ten Preachers* (Nashville: Abingdon, 1991).

The basics of scriptural study can be found in John H. Hayes and Carl R. Holladay, *Biblical Exegesis: A Beginner's Handbook* (Rev. ed. Louisville: Westminster John Knox Press, 1987). My recommended study Bible is Wayne A. Meeks, ed., *HarperCollins Study Bible* (New York: HarperCollins Publishers, 1993). There are a variety of biblical concordances out there, though we seem to be lacking Old Testament concordances for the newer translations. Any concordance is fine as long as it is *analytical* — that is, it is not just a list of the English words, but cites the underlying Greek and Hebrew. Those who prefer electronic concordances of

182

the original languages will find the cream of the crop represented by *Bible Windows* for PC and *Accordance* for Mac. For elementary reference books, I commend David Noel Freedman, ed., *Anchor Bible Dictionary* (New York: Doubleday, 1992), and Paul J. Achtemeier, ed., *HarperCollins Bible Dictionary* (New York: HarperCollins Publishers, 1996). A good one-volume Bible commentary is James L. Mays, ed., *HarperCollins Bible Commentary* (New York: HarperCollins Publishers, 2000). For textual criticism, see Bruce M. Metzger, *The Text of the New Testament: Its Transmission, Corruption, and Restoration* (Third ed. New York: Oxford University Press, 1992) and Ernest Wurthwein, *The Text of the Old Testament: An Introduction to the Biblia Hebraica* (Second ed. Grand Rapids: Eerdmans, 1995). Specific text-critical evaluation of key passages is found in Metzger's *A Textual Commentary on the Greek New Testament* (Second ed., Minneapolis: Fortress Press, 1995).

Model biblical interpretation for the preacher is found in Luke Timothy Johnson, *The Writings of the New Testament* (Rev. ed., with the assistance of Todd C. Penner. Minneapolis: Fortress Press, 1999). Johnson spells out the implications of his method for the Church in *Scripture and Discernment: Decision Making in the Church* (Nashville: Abingdon Press, 1996). Model exegesis even more geared to the preaching moment is again available thanks to the Chalice Press reprint of Gail O'Day, *The Word Disclosed: John's Story and Narrative Preaching* (St. Louis: CBP Press, 1987); O'Day's approach is also illustrated in her commentary on John in vol. 9 of *The New Interpreter's Bible.* Another approach to the relation of the Bible and the Church which will be of help to the preacher is Sandra M. Schneiders, *The Revelatory Text: Interpreting the New Testament as Sacred Scripture* (San Francisco: HarperSanFrancisco, 1991). On one particular point: James Barr's article " 'Abbâ,' isn't 'Daddy' " is found in *Journal of Theological Studies* 39 (1988): 28-47; a summary accessible to the nonspecialist is " 'Abba, Father' and the Familiarity of Jesus' Speech," *Theology* (1988): 173-79. My own exegetical work for the pulpit is found in *If a Sermon Falls in the Forest: Preaching Resurrection Texts* (Lima, Ohio: CSS Publishing Co., 2002) and in recent issues of *Emphasis: A Preaching Journal for the Parish Pastor* (also from CSS).

The structure of the sermon has been addressed by a number of homiletical works; in addition to Craddock's *Preaching*, the foremost include Ronald J. Allen, *Interpreting the Gospel: An Introduction to Preaching* (St. Louis: Chalice Press, 1998), David Buttrick, *Homiletic: Moves and Structures* (Philadelphia: Fortress Press, 1987), Thomas Long, *The Witness of Preaching* (Louisville: Westminster John Knox Press, 1989), Eugene L. Lowry, *The Homiletical Plot: The Sermon as Narrative Art Form* (Expanded ed. Louisville: Westminster John Knox Press, 2000), Charles L. Rice, *The Embodied Word: Preaching as Art and Liturgy* (Fortress Resources for Preaching. Minneapolis: Fortress Press, 1991), Thomas H. Troeger, *Imagining a Sermon* (Abingdon Preacher's Library. Nashville: Abingdon, 1990), and Paul Scott Wilson, *The Four Pages of the Sermon* (Nashville: Abingdon, 1999).

Those interested in oral style can benefit from a classic on written style, William Strunk, Jr., and E. B. White, *The Elements of Style* (Fourth ed. New York: Allyn & Bacon, 1999). More help on grammar can be had amusingly from Karen Elizabeth Gordon, *The New Well-Tempered Sentence: A Punctuation Handbook for the Innocent, the Eager, and the Doomed* (Rev. ed. New Haven: Ticknor & Fields, 1993), and *The Deluxe Transitive Vampire: The Ultimate Handbook of Grammar for the Innocent, the Eager, and the Doomed* (Updated ed. New York: Pantheon Books, 1993), though her constructions are a bit too baroque to be imitated in an oral style. Style is best learned by reading the greats; the place to start is V. S. Pritchett, ed., *The Oxford Book of Short Stories* (New York: Oxford University Press, 1981) or Joyce Carol Oates, ed., *The Oxford Book of American Short Stories* (New York: Oxford University Press, 1992), while the place to continue is Clifton Fadiman and John S. Major, *The New Lifetime Reading Plan* (Fourth ed. New York: HarperCollins Publishers, 1999). The preacher could also do well to have on the shelf for ready reference — in addition to a good dictionary and thesaurus — Bartlett's *Familiar Quotations* (Justin Kaplan, general editor. 16th ed. Boston: Little, Brown and Company, 1992) — just make sure you become familiar with the literature and the history behind the quotations!

Specific help with oral style in preaching is found in Richard Carl Hoefler, *Creative Preaching and Oral Writing* (Lima, Ohio: CSS Publishing Co., 1978), and G. Robert Jacks, *Just Say the Word! Writing for the Ear* (Grand Rapids: Eerdmans, 1996). Jacks's book is particularly helpful in training oneself to distinguish between oral and written styles, and is well worth working through, though the written style of the book is somewhat off-putting. Delivery issues, with special reference to the connection between preaching and acting, find coverage in Jana Childers, *Performing the Word: Preaching as Theatre* (Nashville: Abingdon, 1998); those who need to work on vocal production issues should start with Childers. I am indebted to Eugene Lowry for his title, *Doing Time in the Pulpit: The Relationship Between Narrative and Preaching* (Nashville: Abingdon Press, 1985).

The preacher looking for different approaches to working without a net may profit from Joseph Webb, *Preaching Without Notes* (Nashville: Abingdon, 2001), which draws on a classic in the field, Charles W. Koller, *Expository Preaching Without Notes* (Grand Rapids: Baker Book House, 1962; reprinted as *How to Preach Without Notes,* 1977). I have presented an alternative in this book, but I doubt that one method will work for everyone. Ultimately, you have to find your own style on the tightrope.

Finally, preachers interested in congregational feedback should read Ken Untener, *Preaching Better: Practical Suggestions for Homilists* (New York: Paulist, 1999). This Roman Catholic bishop wanted to know how his priests were doing in the pulpit, so he went out to the congregations and asked! His copious notes form the basis of this helpful little book.

CPSIA information can be obtained at www.ICGtesting.com
Printed in the USA
LVOW01s1805081113

360566LV00003B/313/P